The Spirit for Travel

The Spirit for Travel

Auram Smith

PARTRIDGE
A Penguin Random House Company

To order additional copies of this book, contact
Partridge India
000 800 10062 62
orders.india@partridgepublishing.com

www.partridgepublishing.com/india

Contents

Dedication

I dedicate this novel
To my Family,
They provided me everything,
They gave me
The life
And
They taught me
To be
A
Wonderful
Human being

Acknowledgement

I thank my grandfather, for providing me knowledge.

I thank my grandmother for all her sweets and gossips.

I thank my father, mother and my sister for providing me a great LIFE.

I thank my friends and relatives for providing me a great childhood.

I thank my Guide for the time.

I thank my teachers for encouraging me.

I thank my phone Nokia XL, Google maps, Google Chrome, Idea Internet, Airtel Internet, Pixlr Express, MS word and my HP laptop.

I thank B.Parthiban for clicking the picture

I thank the Publishing Company for publishing my first book.

And finally

I thank the readers for buying this book.

About The Author

The author is a Veterinarian.
Has great passion towards animals.
Loves to write and travel.

Preface

Travelling has become the most
important part of our day to day life.

It is not just an act of moving from one
place to other, geographically.

For some it is the way of finding their true self.
LIFE to me Means:
Love, Individuality, Faith, Empathy
KNOWLEDGE IS POWER
MIRACLES DO HAPPEN

Prologue

"BhO ShambO Shiva SambO SvayambO."

He heard the sound of the song, he ran to see from where that vibrant ecstatic sound of the song oozed. He ran to the Thillainathar shrine and there he saw her, clad in a green sari with a thin red streak on her forehead. Her eyes closed, lost herself to the formless lord, her hands swinging and her vocals singing with great passion.

He stared at her, never took his eyes off. The song had a great positive vibrant effect. It made his heart filled with happiness and his mind with goodness.

As a traveler, he travelled across the world and lived ages to tell a tale. The thing is, no matter how far you travel, one has to come back to the place where it all started, Chidambaram.

He stood motionless, lost in deep thoughts. Listening to the song, tears flooded his eyes, he was happy for no reason.

There was a huge crowd around her, after Amirtha finished singing, she left the shrine and he followed her, he told her that he had fallen for her. He gave her a lotus flower but she was struck with embarrassment but she looked at him with astonishment. She walked away without taking the flower.

He took up the job of a postman in Chidambaram, stayed in a village nearby. He came to all her recitals to woo her but Amirtha saw him only as a stalker.

On the 9th Naatiyanjali function, he saw her dancing bharathanatiyam. He was completely enchanted by the way she danced.

One fine day Amirtha and her friend Leela went to Thirumanangeri temple. She was given a sacred yellow thread as a blessing. Amrita kept the sacred thread in her purse safely.

On the 11th Naatiyanjali function Amirtha and her friends Leela and Ganesh were performing bharathanatiyam, Ganesh sprained his leg, he was not able to perform, Amirtha needed a backup dancer, but then help came in the form of the postman. He told her that he can help her.

He convinced Amirtha that he can dance bharathanatiyam and also other classical dances. Amirtha looked at him with an eye of doubt but the situation was not in her favor. Amirtha agreed to let him dance. He danced in accordance to the raagam and thaalam. Amirtha had an eye on him the whole time watching his every move as she danced.

At the end of the dance Amirtha was uncontrollably happy; she fell in love with him. She embraced him on the stage in front of everyone gathered there. She ran off the stage to get the sacred thread that she had in her purse. She told him to marry her. They both got married happily on stage.

Their happiness didn't last forever. Amirtha reached the gates of heaven after giving birth to her son Mithun. Amirtha's mother and father took care of the child. Amirtha's husband got promoted to post of post master.

Mithun's father took Mithun to a lot of places. He told Mithun lot of stories which gave him a wild and wide imagination. Mithun was very inquisitive as he wanted to know and gain more knowledge.

"So what is this Chidambara Raghashiyam?" Mithun asked his father in an inquisitive tone.

"It is up to you to find out my son." His father smiled.

Mithun was so attracted to the ancient myths. He had a strange attraction towards the secret underground pathways of the forts and temples; he wanted to unravel the secrets that they held. Mithun loved his father very much. He never felt like he lost his mother.

His grandmother and grandfather told him a lot of mythical and moral stories which mostly shaped his character. His mind was fixed with three things.

Never hurt others, physically or mentally.

Never steal or feel jealous of others.

Always fight for the truth and help the people in need.

Mithun followed his grandparents closely. He was heartbroken when his grandparents passed away in an accident. Only Mithun and his father survived the crash.

Mithun wanted to be an archaeologist and after completing a Bachelor Degree in History, he told his father he wanted to do Archaeology in Thanjavur.

Chapter – 1

Travel Begins

01

TRAVELLING has always been Mithun's passion, the moment he gets into a car, bus or a train he feels like a great adventure is ahead of him. In his younger days travelling was all about roads, the vehicles and speed but later it turned out to be exploring new places and meeting new people. As he grew up his interest turned in to travel and archaeology.

He visited most of the places that he read in his history books during his school days.

His interest for travelling and love for history made him to take up post graduation in history and archaeology at the University of Thanjavur.

His father gave an address of his friend's son Vinayagam, who lived in Thanjavur to help Mithun with good accommodation. Mithun got off from the bus, looked around the busy bus stand for Vinayagam. Thanjavur was a big and busy city, thoughts were running inside Mithun's mind, new city, new friends, new life, a new beginning and a new adventure, all together excited him.

He took out his cell phone and dialed the number on his outdated Nokia 101, Vinayagam on the other side, who was driving his bike halted to the side of the road then took his phone from his pocket and answered the call.

"Hello Mithun, have you reached the bus stand?" before Mithun could answer the words came "I'll be there in 5 minutes, wait in-front of the Vasantha Bhavan restaurant." He said in a hurried tone.

Mithun said "Ok".

Mithun found the restaurant and started walking towards it, the bus stand was very busy and he saw the bus ready to leave for Trichy and people were rushing here and there to get their respective buses.

"Welcome to Thanjavur." He saw a big board, he felt like he had a deep connection to the city, something like a mystery yet a magical connection which seemed to be slightly confusing.

A black pulsar 150 cc passed him. Mithun guessed it must be Vinayagam.

Vinayagam was in his early 30s wearing a glass, thin framed, lean. The hair was little grayish. He parked his bike in front of the restaurant and called Mithun on his phone, Mithun saw him taking out his phone and dialing, Mithun marched towards him and introduced him.

"Mr. Vinayagam?"

"Hi, Mithun, nice to meet you, come on lets have some good filter coffee".

They both entered into the restaurant and took a seat near the entrance, they sat facing the road, and the waiter came hurriedly Vinayagam ordered coffee and started to talk about the details of how his family knew Mithun's family.

The waiter kept the coffee on the table. Mithun started to sip his coffee. The coffee had a good taste, it was refreshing and he liked it very much. Mithun finished the coffee very soon he was waiting for Vinayagam to finish, Vinayagam paid the bill, took him to visit the place where Mithun was going to stay.

Vinayagam explained about the place and he said that the house owner is his old friend and school mate. Mithun spoke to the house owner. Mithun introduced himself and told about his study and the period of stay. Vinayagam got the room key and took him to the stairs. The look of the upstairs was astonishing; there was a nice garden in front of his room.

The room was small, can normally fit two people comfortably. There was a shelf and nothing much, the roof was made up of Mangalore tiles. The bathroom and toilet were clean; Mithun was happy and thanked Vinayagam for helping him out.

"Do you like it?"

"Super."

Vinayagam then took Mithun to the mess nearby, told him to take food at the mess and assured him the food is good there. He took him to the shop for buying him mattress, bed sheet, mug, bucket and a mirror. Vinayagam dropped him back at his room and told him not to hesitate for asking help and come home whenever possible.

Mithun reached back to his room placed the bag in a corner of the room. Mithun called his father and told him everything went fine and he was going to take bath. Mithun stepped out of the bathroom came to his room, opening the door, which made a kreech sound, he took the towel from his waist, dried himself and Mithun wore a grey T-shirt and a brown ¾ trouser.

He locked his room, walked towards the mess.

"This is the place I'm going to stay for two years", he thought as he walked. He reached the mess, he saw the board glittering in light it was written in big black bold letters as "Shardha mess", he went inside, sat on the table. The mess was a small square room, painted green and the parotta master was beating up the dough and there was an old man who seemed to be the cashier.

"What do you want to eat sir?"

"4 parottas."

"4 parottas" shouted the old man to the parotta master. The old man placed a plate on the table and covered it with a banana leaf, placing water near it.

The parottas were served hot, the kurma poured all over the parotta. Mithun ate well and paid the bill, he walked back to his room slowly enjoying each foot he placed on the earth.

The registration for the classes was tomorrow and Mithun was eager to meet new people, he started writing his dairy as he left out a loud yawn, he kept the dairy on the table and prepared his bed with the newly brought mattress and started wondering about the new friends he's going to make.

The new adventures he's about to venture, all the excitement which made him awake, he slept after a time that he did not remember when.

02

It was a bright sunny day and the city of Thanjavur was busy, Mithun was already late for college, he rushed for the mess and took some idilis and ran to the bus stop. The bus stop was densely crowded and he was standing in the corner waiting for his bus, the wait was like 5 minutes, then came the bus totally crowded, Mithun managed to get inside the bus and took a ticket. He felt like it was a big achievement, not yet screamed the inner voice; he has to get down at the correct stop in this heavily crowded vehicle.

Mithun was keenly watching all the bus stops, even though after the conductor assured Mithun that he will inform him when the bus reaches the college bus stop. Mithun did not want to miss the spot and be late for the registration. Mithun always had a thrill for getting things done at the last moment. It gave him a sense of excitement in life. The bus reached the college bus stop, the conductor waved his hand pointing Mithun, with a lot struggle he managed to get down from the bus, he saw the university gate and he walked towards it.

He felt happy but mixed with an emotion of fear. Mithun entered into the gates. He was stopped by the security inside the gates for identification. Mithun managed to get into the college and to his department by asking the way from the security. The excitement was rushing through his veins, as he entered his department. He thought there would be a huge strength of students. All the excitement waned off as he saw only two people in the department.

He felt like he had come very early, but later he came to know that there were only four students including him. He was wondering about the odds and finally he came to a conclusion that UG is nothing compared to PG. The students were called inside the HOD room and they were asked to introduce themselves.

"Excuse me", came a voice from behind, the voice was so sweet, Mithun turned back to see an angel coming inside the door swiftly with all smiles. It all happened in slow motion. The beautiful smile he had ever seen.

The students introduced themselves to each other and they were asked to go for the orientation programme. The girl who came late introduced her to the others, she was Shobitha, Mithun stole quick glances at her and then they went along with the professor for orientation, other department students also joined them. In the evening they were asked to come to the main auditorium. Mithun went inside the auditorium, it was a welcome party.

Mithun had never seen such a huge welcome party. As the event proceeded, there was so much excitement, students singing their favorite song, some mimicking the actors.

Mithun was called on to the stage "Vanakkam." Mithun said. The crowd jeered which so much applause. Mithun introduced himself politely and came down from the stage.

Then a fair girl came over the stage, who just cooed something "la la laa!" like music but it was very good. It was a song from Shakira's album and Mithun was thrilled by the way she sang but he failed to get her name and the details of the song, he was lost in his wild imagination.

The girl was very beautiful. Mithun was speechless by her amazing talent.

Then it was one of Mithun's colleagues who went on to the stage and sang the famous song from the movie Sivaji and there was a big mass of applause.

Shobitha was on the stage and introduced herself, Mithun was listening to her each and every word very keenly, she sang the song "ANBAE VA EN MUNBAE VA", and that instant Mithun knew she was the girl.

Many had the same thoughts like Mithun but Mithun had an upper hand, since she was his classmate. She was the star of the day. She enchanted the university with her voice. Mithun praised her heartily the next day.

The classes started, there were lot of minor subjects for others and the class was pretty crowded. Mithun used to steal glances at Shobitha. Shobitha never looked at him.

As the classes proceeded, a conference was announced and students were asked to participate, the students were assigned to form groups and they have to present on a topic they like to work on and one from the group has to present it in front of the judges. Mithun could never forget that day, the day Shobitha spoke to him on her own, it was all slow motion and sweet music to him, and he nodded to whatever she spoke.

She was kind of bossy but Mithun liked her attitude. Mithun and the group worked on the topic of Indian myth and precisely about the plagiarism of the Indian myth in other myths. Mithun did not have a laptop, Shobitha helped him in assisting and he was good at the

Indian myth and they spent more time together preparing for the presentation.

03

The conference day, the spirit for enthusiasm was on the air and everyone dressed as if they were attending a royal marriage festival. The conference hall was decorated very grandly. At the reception stood two beautiful girls clad in similar pink silk sari and then came Shobitha in a beautiful cotton sari, it was green with golden floral borders, Mithun was dumbstruck by her beauty, Mithun was in a white full hand shirt and a black pant and he wore a blue tie.

Mithun felt nervous as Shobitha gained on him, he could smell the shampoo from her hair which escalated his feelings.

Shobitha gave him a handshake and the moment he touched her hand for a shake he felt shaken in his heart.

His heart was pounding like it was going to explode. He looked deeply into Shobitha's eyes for a sign. Shobitha's hand felt very soft, Mithun never felt anything as soft as that, it was so velvety, Mithun had to let it go, all of this lasted for just half a minute. Shobitha gave him the pen drive which had the presentation and she wished him luck and she walked past him. He looked at her, he thought she would turn back, relating to a movie notion but this is reality no such things happen.

Mithun's turn at the presentation, Mithun searched for Shobitha, it was default for him. He saw Shobitha smiling and it gave him courage, he was proceeding with the presentation and he saw people looking else were, talking but he saw Shobitha sitting upright and listening to him with her eyes focused on him. Mithun did the presentation extremely well.

Everybody applauded, Shobitha patted him on his back and stood close to him, Mithun felt bit excited and shy.

It was obvious that Mithun and his team got the first prize. Mithun also got the best presenter prize. Shobitha was standing near him. He looked at her, flashes everywhere flashing from the camera at him and his team, he closed his eyes. He wanted that moment to freeze, Shobitha standing so close to him. He was happy that he was able to impress Shobitha and all the others present but it was Shobitha he wanted to impress.

Mithun felt her sari brushing him slightly when she crossed him. Mithun was lost in his own dream world. He saw his gorgeous, clad in the green sari, observing her every move from the tingling of her ear rings to the movement of the sari border over her toe. The whole world stopped for him, it was all in slow motion when he started to look at her.

Mithun was excited to go to college and he loved college more than any place in the world. Shobitha would come by the bus and he would be waiting there for her every day. He would talk to her and she would often smile at him and he would look in to her eyes and he felt blissful.

Shobitha was sad and did not talk to anyone properly. Mithun felt that she might have sensed his intention for her. He felt like that she started to maintain a distance mentally. Mithun was feeling bad but Shobitha was back to normal by the next week.

Then came the inter college sports meet, Shobitha was the captain of the girls Kho-Kho team and Mithun came to the ground and he saw Shobitha standing in the ground along with her team, they were all in a blue jersey. Shobitha looked stunning.

Mithun could not take his eyes of her athletic curves, Shobitha gave him a surprise anger look in return, Mithun had a sudden jolt in his heart, he put his head down, Shobitha saw him and continued on her game, Mithun looked at her she was running and chasing the other team girls and she was winning, Mithun went to the slow motion mode, he saw her sweat running from the forehead to the nose and she was blowing the drop of sweat from the tip of the nose. She was all game, she was a lioness hunting its prey, it was then the time for the next team to chase, Shobitha coordinated her team and they played very well and reached the finals.

The final match was very interesting, Shobitha injured her leg as she fell down, Mithun was shocked and he ran towards her. Before he could reach her she stood up and the substitute was called on to continue the game.

Shobitha was walking towards the first aid committee, she went a little off balance and she leaned her hand and Mithun held her hand firmly and he praised her for the spirit in her, she sighed. She was taken for first aid, the girl there washed the bruise which was covered with mud and then applied tincture, Shobitha held Mithun's hand tighter than ever. She told him that the tincture hurts, Mithun was happy that it did. He couldn't sleep, he was ruminating his memory of touch and about the clasp of Shobitha's hand.

04

Shobitha and Mithun became inseparable friends, they were always chatting and discussing. Mithun fell in love with her more and more as the days passed. It was Shobitha's birthday and she came in light blue sari, she looked like an angel, Mithun got her a gift and she opened it and it was a green hand bag, Shobitha was flattered, the bag had some small gifts inside and some notes.

Shobitha was pondering over the bag; she was lost in examining the bag, Mithun saw her state and he was on cloud nine, what is more satisfying when the one you love is happy.

Mithun had another sleepless night and he thought so much about proposing to her but his inner voice said that she'll accept, but his other side told him she is not an object to give her heart to you just because you gave a gift to her. Mithun thought for a long time and this seemed to be the right thing.

She is my best friend. He wrote the sentence in his journal and then closed it. He tried to get some sleep.

Shobitha did get a hint, she had feelings for him but she only remained as a friend but she too thought about it, she wanted him to come and propose to her but never happened.

Mithun became addicted to her and intoxicated by her eyes. The college days passed like passing clouds they were quick. It was like yesterday but Mithun was preparing hard for the final exams resisting very hard. His urge to see her was like a forest fire. Mithun did not talk well to Shobitha on his last days of college.

Mithun had to get good grades to secure his future. It was the time for the farewell party.

Mithun took snaps with Shobitha and both were sad but they acted like they were happy.

It was all cameras and flashes. Mithun and his close friends bid goodbye. It was time for Mithun to face reality and the responsibility of life. His untold love was a heavy burden and the biggest secret he kept which was only known to him and his diary. He thought to unveil it after getting a good job. He came out of college with a heavy heart.

Two years of college passed all a sudden. Mithun woke up in the same room. It was all a good experience and Vinayagam became his best buddy. Mithun did not want to leave Thanjavur; he found the place to be much better than his own home. The fear of facing the real world also taunted him. Vinayagam came to Mithun's room in an auto rickshaw. Mithun kept his things in the auto and they both left for the bus stand. It was time for Mithun to leave Thanjavur. Mithun had already sent his things through parcel by train to his home. Vinayagam patted Mithun's back and made him feel comfortable.

"I'll be missing you very much", said Mithun.

"Me too, my friend", replied Vinayagam.

The auto reached the bus stand and he was all set to go to is home. Mithun boarded the bus with a heavy heart, the bus to Chidambaram started moving and Vinayagam waved his hand, saying bye and in response Mithun waved his hand.

05

Mithun took the seat adjacent to the driver, observing the roads through the wind shield, the sound of the engine and the rhythmic changes of the gear were the music for Mithun on the road. The roads seemed to be calm in the early hours of morning, buses and cars passing on each side now and then. Mithun felt like sleeping, but he was watching through the windshield.

He made an attempt to talk to the driver by saying that he is driving at very average speed. The driver told him he must keep his speed average so that the fixed mileage can achieved otherwise he will be given a penalty.

So the driver had no option other than to maintain his speed and not to fall behind the schedule time. The driver and Mithun started talking, the bus moved and the trees moved backwards. Then Mithun's mind started to think of his responsibilities, his future and his work and about his untold love. He began to worry about the job he was going to take up.

The bus reached Kumbakonam and the driver decided to have a coffee, the driver called him to have coffee with him, Mithun refused politely. But the driver insisted and they shared some chitchats. After coffee they went back to the bus.

They started from Kumbakonam, the bus was speeding up, and Mithun was glancing through the window aimlessly. Thinking about his old college days, munching the happy memories, smiling to himself inside in his head, he felt happy about his days in Thanjavur. He always had an ethnic link to the city of Thanjavur, Mithun could not understand the ecstatic feeling the city brought him when he had his foot on the soil of Thanjavur.

The bus entered into Mayiladuthurai bus stand, the bus would stop there for half an hour, so Mithun decided to have his breakfast and he looked at his watch.

It was a Titan fast track which was gifted by Shobitha, he walked out of the bus stand went to the Anandha Bhavan restaurant.

The restaurant was shady as it was an old restaurant; the road was very narrow only a bus could fit. He sat behind the billing table.

The server came fast, he started listing the items for Mithun to order, Mithun ordered idilis, the server jotted with a ballpoint pen on a small piece of notepad and gave a loud cry. Mithun went to wash his hands and he came back just in time for the idilis, the idilis were hot, the server poured some sambar and chutney, he kept his hand over the idilis and he started to taste it by dipping it in the chutney, it was delicious and after that he ordered a cup of coffee, which edged his breakfast.

Mithun went to pay the bill, he walked out of the restaurant, he saw a middle aged lady with a big framed spectacles begging for food, she saw Mithun and asked him if he could get her some idilis, the first thought that hit Mithun's mind was like whether gods were testing him? So he ordered a parcel of idilis, "idilis were done." replied the server. Mithun asked the lady whether she would mind if he got her dosa instead of idilis.

He gave her the packed rolled dosa. She called him near and blessed him with her hands placed on his head. Her blessed words made Mithun to wonder. Mithun really felt happy and wonderful though he had a guilt that it was his father's money but still he was determined that he did a good job. He returned back to the bus and sat on his seat just in time for the driver to arrive and start the bus.

Mithun was thinking about his act of kindness and the state of mind he present in that moment of that act of kindness he performed earlier.

Did God just came in disguise to test my integrity, is this how the wheel of life runs, the worldly force that helps us during the hardships is directly proportional to the help we render to the world, as he was lost in his thoughts, he leaped to the front and held the seat handle tightly with his palms, the driver suddenly applied the brakes.

There was a heavy traffic. There was a long line of vehicles. Mithun got down from the bus to see what the problem was.

He saw a private bus standing in the centre of the road blocking the way for both side vehicles to pass. There was a big quarrel. The bus stood there for nearly 20 minutes. Mithun went side ways to attend nature's call and then he walked towards the parked bus, to listen to the problem.

He called his father and informed him that there is some quarrel going on in the road between two buses and told him that he will be late to reach home. It was about the clash between a private and a college bus; the college bus driver didn't slow down for the private bus while overtaking but still the private bus overtook the college bus. It could have been a very dreadful accident.

The private bus driver got furious and parked the bus across the college bus blocking the road, Mithun thought of sneaking into the bus and driving it, so that the road won't be blocked anymore. Mithun clenched his jaws for being impotent on the situation. There was a long line of vehicles and then the police was called, they came rushing to the site and they solved the issue, Mithun got back to the bus and the bus started to move.

The driver was very irritated, he cannot be there in time and he had to explain this to the higher officials for not being on time. Mithun felt this journey to be unusual, but found it to be interesting. Are there more surprises in store for the journey, Mithun's heart paced and the bus started speeding. There were many sharp turns on the way towards Sirkazhi. The road was a little bumpy and uneven though the driver did not bother, the bus was speeding up in the turns and it was a bumpy ride. The bus reached the border of the Vaitheeswarankoil and Mithun saw a big crowd of people with their animals especially the government goats and two people wearing white coats, he saw a giant hanuman statue and wished by folding hands as the bus crossed the Ramar temple.

The bus entered the bus stand and stopped for two minutes. There was a straight road that went directly to the temple and another sharp right turn and a left turn. The turn had a Vinayagar temple on the left side, the bus took the sharp right turn there was a stopping there to the left of the right turn and people got in to the bus.

It was a straight road to Sirkazhi from Vaitheeswarankoil which connects to the highway, the bus entered in to the Sirkazhi town. A girl came running towards the bus, she seemed like a foreigner. She looked African. She was beautiful. She was in a T-shirt and jean. Mithun wondered what she would be doing here.

She boarded the bus. She sat behind Mithun. She asked for a ticket to Chidambaram, the conductor asked for 16 rupees, she did not have change and all she had was thousands, the conductor stressed on the word change. Hearing the conversation Mithun turned to have a look at them.

Like helping the damsel in distress Mithun spoke to her about resolving the problem by buying the ticket for her and told her she can give the change to him later.

He got the ticket for Chidambaram and gave it to her. She was so happy and thanked him by repeating the words "thank you".

She gave her number to Mithun and said she'll repay him as soon as she gets the change. Mithun asked her details and about her visit. He came to know her name is Ngel and she is from America and she came here on writing an article about the superstitious belief prevailing in the country. She stays in a women's hostel in Chidambaram.

She'll be staying there for a period of time to study the whole state. They soon became good friends on the journey and since Mithun is an archaeology graduate he told her more about the country.

The bus was travelling in an average speed which felt like a cradle. Mithun fell asleep like all the other in the bus. The bus stood still and Mithun slowly opened his eyes, he was in his hometown, it was Chidambaram, Ngel was calling his name and she said she'll call him and bid goodbye.

♠♠♠♠

06

Mithun called his father on his cell phone and his father arrived on time. His father greeted him and then took him home. His father worked as the post master in a nearby village.

He has to leave from Chidambaram everyday early in the morning and he gets back in the evening. Mithun was his only son and so he never went against his wishes.

But the fear of his future always haunted him, he wanted him to be successful and live a content life.

Mithun stayed in his home doing nothing rather than watching T.V and hanging out and watching movies.

A month passed just like that. Mithun's father told him that he has got a job for him inside the city, in a super market for computer billing. Mithun did not show any interest

Mithun did not show much interest in the social network but now he thought of creating a Facebook account and so he took out his laptop, connected his data card and went to the browser and started the process of creating the FB account.

He created the account and he searched for the one person he wanted to be with, he typed her name and then he found the picture to get his heart broken in to a million pieces, the untold love of her life is with someone else. Looks like her engagement. Mithun felt heartbroken and he could not believe his eyes, it was just a month after college and she is already getting engaged. Mithun felt like fainting, he felt his world becoming dark.

He was completely in shock and he was sweating like a pig, unable to cry, unable to swallow the saliva. He looked at the picture closely and he thought of calling her. He picked up his phone and called her but there was no answer. Mithun did not give a request he logged off and went to the bathroom.

Mithun's father called him to have his breakfast; Mithun joined his father and told him that he is willing to work in the supermarket for the time being. His father felt something was wrong.

He kept some more idilis on Mithun's plate and told him to eat well. Mithun's father left him in the house and started to the post office. Mithun felt like a big coward for not telling his love when he had his chance, he withheld the thoughts of what others will think of him.

Mithun locked his house, walked towards the bus stand and boarded the town bus to Chidambaram; it was a ten minute journey. He felt that travelling will reduce the stress, he reached Chidambaram bus stand, he went up straight to the tea shop and asked for a coffee, behind came a voice saying "Anna, two coffees".

Mithun looked back at them they were two men one was in T-shirt and wearing a Dhoti with strange blue drawstring bag. He was abnormal in his sense of clothing.

The other guy was fair and little bit bulky and he was wearing normal attire but both had colored their foreheads with viboothi and kunguman.

Mithun felt them to be strange and it seems that they were not from this place.

They were conversing in English. The guy with the blue bag took the coffee and called out the name "Ramesh, here take the coffee da". The guy with the blue bag took his coffee and started chitchatting with him in English and this time Ramesh said

"Hey Ram, why don't you ask someone for the way to go to Pichavaram da"?

Ram approached Mithun and asked him "Anna how can we reach Pichavaram"?

Mithun said "You have to catch the town bus from here which will come here in 15 minutes".

"Thanks na" replied Ram.

Mithun thought for a moment and he too decided to go to Pichavaram, since it has been a long time he visited.

He told them he too is on his way there.

Mithun introduced himself and he came to know that those two were internship students, working in

Vaitheeswarankoil as internee and both are veterinary graduates.

The bus came, Mithun as usual sat on the conductor seat, Ramesh and Ram sat behind him. The journey was refreshing for Mithun, they reached Pichavaram. Pichavaram, famous for backwater boating and is the second largest mangrove forest in the world, Ram and Ramesh were delighted at the evergreen sight of it, there was a small tower, a canteen, a big parking ground and the boat deck. Ram and Ramesh left Mithun and they went for boating.

Mithun saw the place filled with families, friends and young people and the sight made him sad but the breeze was good enough to make him happy.

He was waiting for the people to gather so that they can share the cost for renting a boat, the Pichavaram boat ride can be a life changing ride in everyone's life.

Mithun saw Ram and Ramesh taking pictures of the forest in the front boat and waving hands at Mithun. Mithun was enjoying the calm and silent cave tree tunnel in the water. It was like a journey to find a rare artifact.

Mithun always wanted an adventurous life but his life was so simple and boring. The boat ride was at a point boring for Mithun as it was just water and the trees and nothing else, the driver turned the boat around and they came to the deck and Mithun paid his share of currency.

Just as he came he saw Ram getting into the bus leading back to Chidambaram, he was calling Ramesh to come soon. Mithun too went to board the bus and so the journey back to Chidambaram.

It was 4.00 PM and somehow Mithun spent his day. Ramesh and Ram bid goodbye to Mithun and they were heading straight to Vaitheeswarankoil.

Mithun came back to his home, washed his feet and opened the door, he felt so tired, he went straight to the bedroom and he fell on the bed.

07

The trumpets were blown to their full sound and Mithun marched towards a big army with forces of horses and elephant. Mithun was killing soldiers mercilessly and his hand was tattooed with the dancing idol of Shiva, he was marching towards a fort to reach a cry of a women were he was stabbed mercilessly by a well built soldier. Mithun woke up suddenly and he looked at the phone, it was 7.22 PM. Mithun realized it was only a dream. He was so confused and what was that he saw. Why the tattoo of the lord Shiva. He felt that he is somehow connected to the dream. The clock struck 8.00 PM; it was Mithun's father knocking the door. Mithun went and opened the door.

His father brought some food from the hotel for dinner. His father spoke of getting a daughter-in-law to end the part of buying food and so that they can eat good home cooked food. Mithun got irritated, he was furious and scolded his father and asked him to leave him alone.

Mithun told his father that he is too young to get married. His father did not speak a word, simply asked him to have his dinner. Mithun could not sleep. His thoughts seemed to lull over the lost love. He took his laptop and logged in to FB and again looked at the face of the women he wanted.

He sent friend requests to some, he looked at the messages and there were lot of welcoming messages on

Facebook. He checked his friend request notification and confirmed them all, he wanted to keep a profile and cover picture and so he started searching for it in his laptop. He found the pictures for both and made them as his profile picture and cover picture.

His phone rang, he walked towards the dining table to get the phone, it was Ngel and she called him to thank him once again.

Mithun invited her to come over to his home for this weekend. Ngel said she would try. Then after saying goodnight to Ngel, Mithun went back to his room to check his laptop, he searched for Ngel. He sent her a request. He thoroughly read her Facebook profile, her pictures, posts and friend list and he came to know much about her.

Mithun felt sleepy and he looked at the phone and it was past twelve so Mithun signed out, shut down his computer and went to sleep.

The rays of the sun brightened the room, Mithun got up, it was his first day for the job, he got up from his bed, fetched the towel from the closet, went straight to the bathroom.

His father was ready with the coffee. Mithun took the coffee sipped it; his father asked him to be patient on the work environment and gave him some advice.

Mithun's father left him at the super market, his father waved his hands, assuring Mithun and encouraging him to work well.

Mithun entered the super market; he introduced himself to the manager there. He was given a new uniform and the rules were explained clearly. No cell phones during work were the most important rule on the list. Mithun agreed and he was assigned to the billing section, Mithun at the start did the job with some interest but the work was tiresome, he felt the job was boring. He had to bill a long list of groceries for the ladies who shop for the home. He met a lot of different peoples and some funny characters. He felt the job to be a tough one, standing all day billing lot of things, all seemed no fun.

It was at the lunch break Mithun's shift was changed for half an hour. Mithun was having his lunch he took his phone and there were 2 missed calls from Ngel, Mithun called her immediately.

Ngel picked up the phone, Mithun apologized that his phone was in silent mode and told her that he was busy at work.

Ngel told him that she is planning to visit the Navagragha temples and she has to collect the origin stories for her articles.

She wanted to book a taxi to take complete tour around the area so she said she wanted his help. Mithun thought for a moment and he said he will get a taxi and he will drive it so he can also act as her guide during the tour. Ngel liked the idea.

Mithun thought of quitting the job so he talked to the manager and called Vinayagam, told him about the plan and asked him to arrange the taxi.

Ngel told Mithun that she had to leave on the next day, Mithun asked Vinayagam to come with the car half way to Chidambaram, so they decided to meet up at Sirkazhi.

Vinayagam reached Sirkazhi by 10.00 PM and Mithun came a little late as he has to do some explaining to his father, they met and Vinayagam gave the keys of the car to Mithun and Vinayagam took the bus to Thanjavur.

Mithun heard the bell sound from the temple; it was from Sirkazhi's Sattainathar temple. It was a special function that took place on every Friday night and he felt like it was a call for him to visit the temple.

A sense of excitement filled Mithun's heart as he started the car and drove off.

He reached the temple and there the whole folk of Sirkazhi had gathered to see the puja. The temple is of three stages and seeing Sattainathar is the final stage in the temple. Mithun went upstairs and looked at the gods Shiva and Parvathi travelling in a Boat, they were in human form and the statue was lively, upstairs to that is the Sattainathar temple, Mithun knelt down to get in to the cave like shrine to see god, he took blessings.

He came out of the shrine and there people were sitting in rows and they were served prasadam, Mithun sat nearby an old women and he tasted tamarind rice followed by curd rice, after finishing the prasadam Mithun went to wash his hands, wore his sandals and then went straight to the car and drove home.

Chapter – 2

The Road Trip

01

It was a bright sunny day in Mumbai after the heavy rain subsided, the sun shined to its full glory, the alarm went on. Neelayadacthci picked up her iphone - 6 and she unlocked her phone by swiping the screen. She checked her Facebook, then took off from the bed, went to freshen up, she came back yawning, took the coffee cup lazily started the induction stove made the water boiling and went to pick up the packet of milk from the door. She made coffee, saw some flash news and went straight for a bath.

It was a big day for Neela, the Daya Arts.inc magazine company in Mumbai has contacted her to work for them.

Neela had passed out from the school of photography just a few weeks back and the magazine was already impressed with the photos she had photographed earlier, she was given a project to capture the festival spirit of South India. Neela came out of her bath changed in to her clothes; she always wore grey T-shirts black jean and bluish shades. She looked stunning in that attire; she always felt the need of comfort rather than the beauty in dressing. She went to see Samba, her dog. She gave him some snacks and she went to make coffee, after finishing breakfast, she took her DSLR camera and her lenses. She took Samba, her Rottweiler and went to fetch her ride, she seemed to like rugged and rough vehicles, and she had a Mahindra THAR and samba jumped in to the front seat as soon as she opened the door.

She kept her bag and camera in the backseat, she sat on the driver seat and started the engine and let it run for a while, she revved up the engine making up the noise and samba started barking. She pressed the clutch, shifted the gear and pressed the accelerator moving the vehicle. She parked it outside and went back to close the gates.

She took the highway to reach the city and the traffic was heavy. The signals were so irritating but she enjoyed driving in the tight traffic, it was more of controlled driving. She reached the magazine office; it was on the second floor of the complex.

The lift was not working. She took samba along with her to meet the manager. She got the advance check and she was told that she has to take care of the expenses but they have arranged the train ticket to reach Madurai. Neela refused the tickets and told them she is going on a road trip all the way towards south India.

The manager was stunned to hear this from a 21 year old girl going on a road trip.

"Are you going alone"?

"No sir I'm taking samba, my dog with me".

The manager wished her all the best and Neela took leave from the office. Neela was so excited to go on her first Road trip that too to her native place. Her family origins were rooted to Madurai. Neela was very much interested in meeting them all. She took her THAR and she petted samba and drove towards her home.

She called her dad and told him that she was going on a road trip to south India and she asked for the numbers that she could contact after she reaches south, her father asked her to come visit them before leaving.

Neela, an independent woman, always made her own decisions. She was always good at choosing between what's right and wrong. Her dad was not worried about her going alone but the parenting instinct always had a way of interfering with the freedom.

Neela met her mother and father, she had lunch with them and she said she was leaving the day after tomorrow. She wanted to take complete rest before she goes on her road trip. Her parents had no chance rather than letting her go. Neela had a plan and it was completely safe. There was no equality among men and women in the country, if any women who wanted to travel alone! It won't be happening in India like compared to the other countries because India is not safe for women, that's what they say. A lot of reports on women trafficking and rape in the country prevails, women are not afraid to travel alone but their parents are and the society has a different view on a girl or a women who travel long way all alone.

This superstitious belief that women should always travel with a companion at this technologically developed century. But still people have to change a lot. It's a forced template on women. Travelling alone on a long distant trip is like not happening.

Neela decided to meet her friend Radha who works as a Doctor in Goa and then she planned to stay with her friend Anita who studies law in Bangalore. This was the plan she had in mind and she crafted them perfectly, she called both of her friends and told them she'll be arriving there.

After lunch Neela bid goodbye to her parents, started her THAR and rode towards her apartment. She wanted to pack her stuff. She took her big trekking bag and stuffed all the needed stuffs for the long travel. She made a check list and did a double check. She then drove off to the Mahindra motor service and checked her vehicle condition, her THAR was hard top and it looked magnificent and nobody thought that a girl would drive such a macho vehicle. The vehicle was in good condition.

She bought an extra can for diesel and filled it at the fuel station. She came home and the next day she completely took rest, spending the whole day inside eating, relaxing and sleeping.

02

The next day she woke up early in the morning got ready as quickly as possible. It was cold and the time was 4.00 AM and she took samba and her things. She checked her house locked it, started the engine turned the music on and began her journey.

The road was little foggy and there were heavy vehicles moving in a line, she drove slowly driving listening the song Mr. Perfect from Arya 2, the beats of the song made her impatient.

She was quite enjoying the music. She drove faster as the beats went faster. She tried to overtake all the vehicles at a single stretch. She was going fast and she felt she had to slow down a bit but the road was deserted so there was no reason for slowing down.

On the way she stopped for chai at the road side tea shop, there was also a taboo that girls don't normally take tea at the roadside tea shops, the country is so different there is no equality in the matter of a single tea.

The tea shop was deserted, the watch on Neela's wrist showed 5.13 AM she rammed the door of her jeep. She walked towards the shopkeeper and asked for a strong tea. The shopkeeper was an old man, he was wearing a brown muffler and he lit the stove, Neela took some biscuits from the big glass bottle and went back to her ride, she opened the door and let samba out and gave some of the biscuits to him.

Samba munched them in a matter of seconds and was asking for more. Neela took her DSLR camera and took some pictures of the tea shop, Chaiwala mixing the tea with the milk from one glass to the other. She captured the facial movement of samba sniffing the biscuit.

Neela walked towards the tea shop to get her tea and the tea tasted very good and she saw some container Lorries stopping by the shop. Neela praised the shop keeper and took some more biscuits and gave one for samba and she was munching one.

The lorry driver came towards the shop and he was scared to shit the moment he heard samba bark, Neela gave the biscuit to samba and pacified him.

Neela took the picture of the Chaiwala and praised the Chaiwala once again for the fine chai and she headed back to her THAR. She started the engine and she checked the fuel gauge, the pointer was pointing full. She looked at the side mirror, moved slowly towards the road. She shifted the gear and she hit full throttle. The THAR was clocking miles on the road like slicing through the iced cake. The sun was coming up and she stopped to see the sunrise.

She always liked the sun rise and this time it was her first long solo road trip, she wanted to capture all the movements and moments. She started to take pictures of samba standing near the THAR along with the sunrise. The picture came out splendid. She along with samba took a selfie.

She uploaded it on the Facebook. She browsed her Facebook timeline for a few minutes and let out a gasp. She locked the phone and opened the door for Samba to get in. She checked the air of the wheels. She started the engine and drove.

She passed Sivaji Nagar. She was driving on the Jeejabai Bhosle Marg road. She took a left turn to catch the Sion Panvel Expressway; it was busy road even in early morning hours. The long bridge was Vashi Bridge. She came to Navi Mumbai; it was a 45 minute drive from Kurla to Navi Mumbai. She was on the Sector 1E. She saw a McDonald's outlet. The shops were closed.

It was only 6.10 AM. She was on the Khanda Colony junction; she took Kalamboli flyover first and then the Mumbai-Pune expressway. It was a long ride. She reached the toll gate. The toll guy took a good look at her and then made a little time in giving the ticket. He said he did not have the change.

Neela had to look in to her bag for change, she gave the change. The gates opened. The THAR roared. The sun rose up shining, spreading the light. She was waiting eagerly to drive over the hilly ghat roads. She felt an adrenaline rush when she saw the road escalating, the THAR was moving in full speed.

She was climbing so fast. She slowed a bit for the ghat road since it was going to end soon if she did the driving at this speed rate. She drove slowly to enjoy the nature, the dense trees, which were a brilliant work of nature.

She stopped by the tiger valley and took some snaps with her camera. She drove towards Khandala. She looked at the time it was 8.00 AM. She felt hungry. She drove, took the NH 4.

She liked the Yumie tummy restaurant which was closer, she reached the hotel and she placed an order for Aloo Parotta and Dahi. It was a great combination of potato with flour when mixed with hard curd, the taste is unique, it made her forget the world, she washed her hands and she started walking towards the jeep, Samba barked, she then remembered that she has forgotten to pay the bill. She was struck with embarrassment.

She made up stories like she had forgotten because of the parotta was very delicious. She took some biscuit and a water bottle, paid the bill. "Good boy samba" she said and gave him a bunch of biscuits. It was 8.30 AM when she looked at the watch and it was a very good breakfast.

She felt energetic. She climbed on to her seat and called samba in. She started the vehicle and drove away.

The weather was cloudy and it was about to rain, Neela loved to drive in the rain. Listening to music adds more delight to the drive while raining. Samba was napping behind the seat; the warmth inside the jeep was perfect. She parked the jeep to the left of the road.

Neela took out the camera and took a few snaps of napping samba and the drizzles that were resting on the Glass of the wind shield. She kept the camera aside the seat and she drove. It started to rain. The drops of rain that fell on the glass created a hazy vision.

The road appeared blurred, Neela turned on the viper, in a single sweep the viper cleared the water, the to and fro motion of the viper with the music inside was like a concert, Neela started to wonder, what is the music of life that drives us. The tires spurting the rain water, the climate was cool and it was dark and so Neela turned on the head lamp, some bikers have halted aside, found some roof to stay away from the rain.

Neela opened the window and felt the rain water through her palms, they were cold and some water splashed on her face, it sent a chill over her body. Goosebumps were all over her skin, rain indeed has an effect of happiness in one's life, she thought while closing the window.

The song "Paani da rang" from Vicky donor was playing and it was an apt song for the situation, her heart felt a sense of great excitement. The guitar strums over the speaker were mesmerizing. She sang the lines along with the song. She looked at the clock, it was 8.55 AM. She was driving on the NH47 and she joined the Mumbai – Pune Expy. The roads were wet and the water sprouting all over, the jeep was a good decision because it was built to get dirty. She decided to drive nonstop till she reaches Kolhapur.

She stepped on the accelerator, the rains were pouring and the THAR was roaring. The song "life Bahut simple hae" from the movie Stanley ka Dabba started to play. Samba woke up and left out a loud yawn. Neela saw him and spoke to him.

"Did you sleep well, samba".

Samba barked in response.

She saw the milestone displaying Warje, just 2 more kilometers to enter in to Pune. It was a three hour ride from Warje to Kolhapur. She drove as fast as she can, the roads started to get boring, since this was the first time she was doing something like this, there was nothing interesting happening. She was bored now.

Except for the music and the rain that were still playing and falling. She felt bad for those drivers who drive alone all around India, goods and other products to earn for their living. She felt pity. She came near the vicinity of Kolhapur, she looked at her phone, it was 2.00 PM in the noon and the rain was still drizzling.

She searched to find a restaurant to eat in Kolhapur, using her phone. She found a McDonalds shop after the Kolhapur mines on the high way. She was in Gandhinagar, she drove across the Uchegoan Lake, there was a Durga Devi temple nearby, she reached the McDonalds shop and opposite to it was KFC, the main reason to choose these restaurants while travelling are they have good clean toilets and they are comfortable. In India it is hard to find each and every hotel having a toilet; though some have, they were highly disgusting.

It was 2.15 PM and still the rain was pouring down, she left Samba in the jeep and went to fetch lunch. There was a huge queue so she had to wait for 15 minutes to get to the counter she took a chicken combo burger and a cheese pizza. She got the bill paid and she gave the order slip. The place was dwelling with youngsters. They were there to get shelter from the heavy rain.

It took 15 minutes more for the order to come up. Finally Neela got her food and she came running to the jeep. She took the chicken burger and took a bite of it. She gave samba some of the pedigree snacks which she had in her jeep. She drove forward. She thought of drawing some money from the ATM.

She was looking out on both sides, she came across a hotel called Jay Hind Dhaba she felt the name to be patriotic and she parked her jeep on the side of the road and took a picture of it.

It was raining, Neela got wet, she ran to the jeep to keep her camera and then ran to the ATM in front of her, she took her purse and took her card, her hand was wet, she dried it by rubbing over her pant, she took the card and swiped it and entered the pin on the touch screen, the AC was at full, she felt the chillness. She entered the amount, the transaction was complete and she counted the money, took the slip, then kept the money in her purse and ran to the jeep and drove.

She crossed the TATA motor showroom as she drove she crossed a big temple Shri 1008 Bhagwan parashwanath Digambar. She was looking for a petrol pump.

She drove a little forward and she found a HP petrol pump. She drove inside the pump. She told the worker there to full the tank with diesel. She gave the money after filling and locked the diesel tank. She was back on the road again; she saw a milk processing unit as she passed by the road. Her phone beeped she looked in to it and saw the message. It was from a friend and it read "PK awesome movie, must watch." She slowed the vehicle banked to the left and googled about the review, the review were all good. She thought she will watch it in Goa.

She got a message in whatsApp and it seemed to be a song from the movie PK and it read "I Love to Waste My Time". Neela downloaded it and she connected it to the speaker, the song began and Neela felt good.

The song had nice music. She reached Kagal. Kagal had a little bit of traffic; she had to maintain her speed under 40kmph. As soon as she reached the outskirts she started accelerating.

She crossed the Doodhganga River and she entered Karnataka – Maharashtra border, the rain was pouring heavily, she came across the Toll Plaza, there was a long line as one of the toll did not work. Neela turned off her music and listened to the rain and looked at Samba, the vehicles in front were moving slowly through the toll gate.

Neela drove to the toll counter and paid the money, got the receipt. The rain was very heavy and she was following the vehicles. They were all going at a stable speed as the rain made a blurred vision of the road and some vehicles were parked to the far left of the road as the indicator lights were blinking.

She overtook the vehicles and she was driving faster, she heard her inner voice telling her to slow down but her instinct was telling her go with her adrenaline rush. She was driving at the speed of 100 kmph. She looked at the speedometer for a second looked at the road and the viper swaying up and down.

She turned on the music again and it was mash up song of Sonunigam. The song was apt for the drive. She slowed down to enjoy the song. She crossed the Veda Ganga River. The road was straight, then came a huge bend to the right and there was a Mahaveer temple and a statue, the road took a bend to the left, in a little while the road was all straight, she reached Kangala, she drove hearing the song "Nenjukulla Ne" from Vadagari.

Samba started barking, Neela thought samba had to attend natures call and so she parked the jeep to the left of the road, Neela opened the door. Samba ran towards a tree nearby.

Neela was feeling the rain, it was heavy and she got inside the jeep. She waited for samba. Samba came barking at her, she got down and took samba to the back of the jeep and dried him and cleaned his dirty paws. She too got wet and changed her dress. She started the engine and drove across the bridge above the Hiranyakeshi River and again the same river and a bridge came, she passed Gotur, and then Chikkalgud.

She drove faster. The rains halted. She reached Hattagiri toll plaza. She paid the money and drove. She was driving at the speed of 100kmph, she crossed the Kittur Rani Chenemma Garden, she took the bottle of water holding the steering wheel in one hand and bringing the water bottle near the other hand to open the cap and she placed the mouth of the bottle on her lips and drank the water and moistened her lips with her tongue, she closed and kept the bottle back.

She looked at samba sleeping at the back of the jeep. She crossed Kakati Hindalco water treatment facility was nearby she saw the facility in awe. She looked at the GPS and she had to take a right and then a left across the ring road. She reached the Indal colony. She took the right under the bridge.

Then came the ring road, she took a left and she pressed the accelerator pedal, she made a praying gesture by folding her hands when she crossed the Vithali Devi

Temple, she drove faster. She passed Belgaum Institute of Medical Science. She came across a four way road and in the center was the Rani Channamma statue, she paused and looked at the GPS and she had to take a right, she took the right and she came across BIG cinemas around Bogarves circle, the theater was crowded, she thought of watching PK movie but she backed up the idea, she reached Gogte were she took a right turn, she was driving across Hindu nagar, Belgaum.

She came to the outer limits of Belgaum and there was a statue of Sivaji. She pulled her vehicle to the far left from the road and took her camera to take pictures of the statue and of the surrounding.

She took a selfie with the Maharaja and drove off. She came across a driving school. She felt nostalgic thinking about her driving lessons and the time she spent in the driving school and the friends she made there, she smiled at herself. She crossed the lush green fields and the livestock, Neela always thought that green is the color of nature and goodness. She liked the color green, even she wanted her jeep to be green but black looked meaner. She was near Halakarni then reached Khanpur, the trees were very dense, she braked and shifted the gear, reducing the speed as the jeep ran over the Speed breaker, it was a railway crossing, she thought how nice would it be to ride in the train into the dense forest filled with green trees.

She came across the Londa high school and came another railway crossing, Neela loved driving in narrow roads with less traffic and trees on both sides. She came to Gharli, she took a sharp right turn and drove as she reached Tinai Ghat, she looked at the time it was 5.08 PM. She thought of having snacks and tea. She parked the jeep nearby, samba was fast asleep she saw a hotel and she went inside the hotel which was full of tourists. She went to the restroom, she came back took a seat and looked at the menu. She ordered for a coffee and some samosa. She took her phone and called her friend Radha and told her that she would be in Goa in an hour or two. She paid the bill; she went to her jeep to start her journey towards Goa. She felt refreshed. She started her THAR and she drove into the astonishing green forest. She drove enjoying the song "Pachai Niramea" from the movie Alaipaayuthey.

The fog was heavy and it became cold all of a sudden. Samba woke up, sat on the front seat. She came across a town called Anmod, she reached the check post. The roads had several bends making the drive interesting. Then came two railway crossings, and she wanted to see the trains cross by but no luck.

Neela passed Mollem. She came across the river Dudhsagar and she reached the place called Kulem, there was a famous waterfall there to which her father had taken her when she was just a child. There was a jeep taxi stand. Neela turned on the headlights. It was dark. She saw a cashew farm and that was Goa. She had to reach Canacona which is further an hour away located in the southern most part of Goa, she rode on the Edapally – Panvel highway crossed Nargocem. She came near the saint Theresa church.

She called Radha and told her that she came to the church. Radha told her to come to the Ruby Residency she will be waiting and sent her the coordinates. Neela set the coordinates and drove to the residency.

03

Radha, a beautiful woman, married to a brave and brilliant Navel officer had recently given birth to her son and her husband had to leave for work.

She lived along with her mother-in-law and her grandma. Radha was from Gujarat. She lost her parents during the earthquake and she met Abishek when he was hospitalized and they became life partners eventually.

Neela's father and Radha's father were partners in business and Radha visited Neela's home for all the vacations. Radha was surprised by Neela's courage to drive all the way from Mumbai. Radha started waving her hand towards Neela.

Samba started barking at Radha and started wagging his tail. Radha petted him Neela and Radha hugged each other. They felt very nostalgic. Neela wanted to meet Radha's son. The three went to the residency and after formal enquiries with Radha's mother-in-law. They all settled down for dinner. Radha's grandma was very busy watching Chotti Bahu serial.

There was loud cry, it was Radha's son and he woke up. Radha's grandma shouted at Radha to watch the kid. Radha got up and took him from the cradle and pacified him and gave him to Neela. Neela was holding him and she was making faces, suddenly the baby urinated on her.

Radha took him from Neela and asked her change the dress. Neela came back after changing her clothes. Radha put her son on the cradle and rocked it.

Radha told Neela about her work. Neela and Radha sat together and tasted some lemon tea and did some catching up. They mostly spoke about the past, the days how they spent playing. Neela was very tired of the driving.

She felt like going to sleep. Radha told her to sleep in the guest room. Neela went to leash Samba. Neela stretched her body and slept on the bed.

Neela was capturing the beautiful nature of Goa it was all blue green and clean, the earth is blue and green together, she thought for a while as she was focusing the boat sailing on the sea, she saw a big wave of tsunami coming right towards the beach, she ran, she was thinking about samba, Radha her son and their family.

The wave hit her hardly and she was drowning, though she put great effort to fight against it, the force of the wave was very strong. Neela heard a faint voice calling her name, her body was aching and her eyelids did not obey her command, after an effort of trying, she woke up and found that she had a horrible dream. It was Radha, she told Neela to brush her teeth and get ready.

Neela rose and went inside the bathroom, she forgot to take her brush, she came back to the room and saw the clock it was 10.00 AM. Neela took the brush and towel and ran into the bathroom.

She came out steaming, the hot water had an effect on her body and it was a good pain relieving bath. She dressed up in a blue Westside T-shirt and a dark blue cotton pant. Radha knocked the door and called her to come and have breakfast. Neela rushed to the dining hall and saw Radha with her grandma watching TV. Radha sat on the table and took the plate and the dish was cylindrical shaped Idilis, she never saw such idilis, Radha came to serve her.

"What are these they look different?" questioned Neela with a surprise.

"They are the same idilis with a different shape, this is famous along these sides and the state Karnataka," replied Radha while pouring some hot sambar.

Neela took a piece of idili and dipped into the sambar and tasted it, it was amazing. Neela appreciated Radha for the tastiest idilis.

Radha told they were made by her mother-in- law and they both had a big laugh, as they both remembered the cooking incident that took place in Neela's home when they were in school.

It was during the annual holidays when Radha came to Mumbai to spend time with Neela, they started cooking tandoori chicken. They put too much masala which made it too spicy and the total lunch was a disaster. They were banned from entering in to the kitchen from that day.

It was about 11.00 AM Radha's son was playing with her mother-in-law. Neela went to fetch her bag and she took a hot wheels toy car and gave it to Radha's son. The baby looked at it for a moment and threw away the toy. Neela took the baby from the floor and kissed him, he started to cry. Radha took him back from Neela told Neela not to scare him, with a naughty smile. Samba started barking, Neela remembered samba was there and she asked Radha whether she fed him, Radha replied in a positive note. She even took samba out for a walk around the colony; Neela smiled at her and told her she's the best.

Neela asked Radha to take her out, the climate was cloudy, Radha decided to take her to the Patnem beach. Radha dressed up in a chudidhar, both went downstairs, Neela went upstairs again to get her camera and back pack, Radha took her Scooty and Neela sat behind. Radha started the bike and rode towards her hospital where she works as a Doctor, she made a U-turn and came back the same way, she passed Chaudi, the Canacona market place, there was lot of resorts, they reached the Patnem beach, the beach was filled with international tourists. Flyers of Goa international film festival were found here and there, Neela remembered that she wanted to watch PK movie and told Radha if she's free then they can go for the movie. Radha entered in to the ocean, placing her foot on the waving water the cold water absorbing the heat from her foot. It seemed to Neela that Radha was meditating.

Neela took her camera and took a beautiful snap of the sea the sky and Radha's foot along with the waves. She was taking snaps of the beach and the ocean in different angles, Radha still eyes closed enjoying the waves massaging her feet. Neela looked at the small crabs burrowing deep in to the beach sand and she snapped them with her camera, she kept her camera and stepped in to the watery waves holding the hand of Radha.

Radha smiled at her. Neela too enjoyed the bliss of standing in the beach sand, her foot washed off by the ocean's waves. They walked along the cost as the waves touched their feet.

"Best stress buster for me," Said Radha.

"It does feel good," replied a giggling Neela.

Radha told her about visiting the wildlife sanctuary tomorrow. Neela's phone rang and it was her mother, she scolded Neela for not calling her. Even once on the way or after reaching Goa. Neela apologized and told she was very tired, that's why she didn't make a call.

She came to know that Radha has informed her about her arrival in the morning. After telling her plans she ended her call.

"So where's the sanctuary?" asked Neela.

"Just a few miles away," replied Radha.

"Thanks for informing my mother about my arrival" said Neela laughingly.

"Not a problem," replied Radha lifting her head up in the air breathing the fresh air.

They walked across the coast on the wet sand. Neela asked her again about PK movie, Radha hesitated a bit; Neela understood and did not push her. They reached back home and the lunch was ready, Radha's mother in law praised samba for being a very good doggie, she told her that she too wanted have a dog but their parents never allowed to have her one.

"Why not now aunty ji?" asked Neela.

Radha's mother-in-law laughed over it, and told Neela to eat well. Radha started laughing. Neela did not understand. They started playing videogames after lunch. It was Need for Speed Carbon, Radha took another game and it was a two player shooting game, then they played Open Season which they quiet enjoyed. Radha got a call from her husband.

Radha rushed out of the room to talk to her hubby, Neela continued to play. It took a long time for Radha to finish talking to her hubby; Neela went to sleep in her room.

Neela closed her eyes and was thinking about the life she's living. She looked at the watch it was 3.18 PM. Neela could not sleep. She heard Radha coming inside the hall. She was in a fix whether to get up or just lie down. Neela woke up hearing a thunderous sound.

She got up went to freshen up and came to the hall searching for Radha. She saw Radha standing in the balcony and enjoying the rain leaning her hand feeling the rain drops, Neela approached her, Radha splashed some water on Neela's face and Neela leaned her hand out and tried to splash water on Radha but she felt another splash of water in her face, before she could react, Radha ran inside, Neela let go of the idea of splashing water and she stared at the rain that poured from the sky. The climate was very cold with rain to add its essence, Neela stood in a self hugging posture, rubbing her arms to warm herself. It was dark and very cloudy; Radha came with two cups of coffee and gave one to Neela.

Neela took the cup, it was hot, the warmth spread over her hand to her body, she took it near her mouth, the expiration from her nostrils made the steam from the cup rise up, she felt the warmth over her face and the smell of the coffee was tempting, she took a sip.

"This is what I was expecting. Radha," said Neela.

"This is BRU ma," replied Radha.

They both laughed at each other.

They could not do anything but to be inside the home as the rain poured down heavily. Radha told Neela that she can't be coming to the wildlife sanctuary, due to the recent change of shift in the hospital. Neela told Radha that she will take the rest of her family with her to the sanctuary tomorrow if it does not rain. Radha agreed. They heard a loud cry, it was Radha's son, and she rushed to nurse him.

Neela's phone rang it was her mother. She went to her room to attend the call. Her mother told her that she and her father are going to London for a business visit and they will be spending their new year there. Neela was repeatedly repeating the word "ok." Her mother said she had deposited some money on her account and told her to ask her if it is not enough.

Neela said she'll checkout. Her mother told her to call her father and talk to him. She then said good bye and disconnected. Neela called her father and she told him about the road trip and the stay at Radha's home. Her father praised her courage and told her drive carefully and slowly.

Neela then asked him about the London trip. Neela's father elaborated his business trip and then told her take care. Neela ended the call after speaking to her father. She came to the hall there she saw Radha's grandma watching serial. Neela sat closer to grandma and started watching the serial, it was a Korean drama. She was watching the subtitle and it was pretty interesting and she found the name of the serial to be Love Lost in Time. There was a series of advertisement; grandma asked Neela whether she watches these dramas.

"No grandma, but I watch a lot of movies, including Korean too." "This drama seems to be interesting, seems like science fiction isn't it?"

"Yes dear, a nice science fiction with a beautiful love story woven around it." Replied grandma

There was a sudden darkness in the house; the current was out. "Oh god" shouted Radha's grandma in the bitterness of not able to watch the end of the drama and in the fear missing the Chotti Bahu serial.

Neela switched on the flashlight from her phone. Radha's mother-in-law came with a lit candle and placed it in the corner of the wall which had a candle holder and then she went inside Radha's room to check on her.

Radha's mother-in-law went back into the kitchen and took some vegetables for cleaning and onions and garlic for peeling. Radha's mother-in-law, grandma and Neela were sitting in the hall; samba started barking at the balcony.

"Is he afraid of the dark?" asked grandma

"Is it true that dogs can see the dead?" asked Neela.

"I don't know about dogs but I think cats can see between the two worlds" said the mother-in-law. They were all cleaning the vegetables in the candle light. Neela tried breaking the garlic and then she started chopping the onion.

"I heard that there are some supernatural entities which help witches and cunning folk during the magic performance and they are called as animal guides or familiars," said grandma in a scary tone.

"I even heard Prince Rupert of England took his dog to the civil war and every time he won it was said that it was because of his familiar spirit. It was said that the dog was killed with a silver bullet" grandma shouted.

"Nonsense, these are just superstition," shouted Radha from the inside of the room. Neela was excited about grandma's story and asked for more.

"Do you know about the witch's milk?" asked grandma.

"No Grandma, tell me," replied Neela. As grandma was about to say the lights flashed and the TV was on, grandma took the remote and switched to the channel to Chotti Bahu. Neela too left the topic and looked the time at the phone, she pressed the unlock button it was 7.04 PM.

Neela's eyes were filled with tears due to chopping the onions, she entered the kitchen and place them on the slab and washed her eyes with water. Radha's mother-in-law cooked a tasty dinner, the rain did not stop and it's Christmas in two days.

04

The next day Neela totally spent her time inside the home, Radha went to hospital, there was nothing much to do for Neela. She took her camera and started snapping grandma and the baby. She then took samba to the parking lot, took pictures of the buildings, the sky and the trees, the birds in the nest and the water that splashed after falling from the sky to the ground.

She started her THAR and rode to the Patnem beach and there people were dancing on the beach, Neela did not want to engage them, she just took snaps of them and drove along, she on the way back found a Maruthi 800 stuck in the mud and she stopped to help them by towing the car with the help of her jeep.

They thanked her and she asked for them to pose for her snap, everybody was smiling and happy. She rode back home and entered the home, Radha's grandma was there in the hall and she looked at Neela and smiled at her.

"Having all the fun alone ha" asked the grandma.

"It was boring grandma here," replied Neela.

"Oh, then what about me?" questioned grandma.

"Shall we go out grand ma" asked Neela.

"Ok, I'll tell you where to go." Grandma said in a dominating tone.

Neela and grandma along with samba got to the jeep and they started, the jeep engine roared, grandma became anxious and started screaming in joy.

They got out of the residency gate, grandma told her to drive to the market and take a right from there, Neela followed but there was no right, she understood that it was a offroading adventure, she let the jeep snuggle in the mud and splatter them around, the rain started pouring heavy and grandma letting out a villainous laugh, Neela felt the adrenalin rush up to her throat and she let them out through her screams through her mouth, she turned in the music and it was Singing "Singh is King", both of them singing the song as the jeep was dancing on the imperfect terrain, then came the railway track, Neela waiting for grandma's permission, were grandma shouted "let's roll".

Neela rode over the train tracks crossing them; the shock absorbers had their effect, both screaming aloud with the rain pouring hard. Neela drove towards the palm trees.

"Forward." shouted grandma.

Neela stepped on the accelerator and they went to the Patnem hill and rode the jeep along the coast of Patnem.

"Faster." shouted grandma.

The rain was pouring heavily and the jeep was splashing the beach sand, they crossed the Patnem beach and reached the Rajbag beach, the people in the beach hut were all surprised to see the jeep travelling at a super speed.

They went near the Talpon river basin.

"Let's wait here for some time" said grandma.

Grandma was looking at the side of the sea and her eyes were full of tears. Neela did not understand the meaning behind the tears and when she tried to ask, grandma wiped her tears and started laughing.

"I still have the spirit for travel and adventure!" grandma said to Neela.

"Yes indeed. Grandma you have the spirit."

"Let's go now kid."

Neela turned the jeep and now they entered the spa resort and drove faster before they could be caught. They reached home. The two sneaked in to the house quietly and grandma resumed the position, Neela decided to take a hot shower and she entered her room.

Neela entered the shower. The hot water fell on her body. She was lost in thoughts about what happened today. She had never done offroading but today it happened, just like that, she was amazed by the spirit that grandma had inside her.

Neela did not want to come out of the shower but Radha came inside the room and shouted at Neela that her mother is on the phone. Neela told her to cut the phone, she take the call after she finishes her bath, Radha told Neela's mother and ended the call. Neela came out of the bathroom wrapped around in a towel; Neela had short hair so there was no problem in drying her hair. She changed in to a t-shirt and a 3/4trouser and took the phone in one hand and throwing the towel on the bed with the other.

She called her mother and spoke about the routine and about the food and all. Radha came in with a cup of coffee. Radha told Neela about her Christmas plan. Neela became excited and proud of Radha's action. It was dinner time. Neela played video games for some time and then she went to sleep.

"Neela, Wake up" shouted Radha.

Neela blabbered something in her sleep, Radha pinched her and Neela gave a kick which nearly missed Radha. Neela got up and Radha pushed her in to the bathroom and locked it, Neela turned on the hot shower and it felt very well, she felt like she could stand there the whole day and even sleep.

Radha started shouting at Neela. Neela came to her senses and she came out quickly and dressed in a blue sari, they went to the church and then straight to the hospital, Neela and Radha had brought cakes for everyone at the hospital. Radha told Neela to distribute them.

They both then headed towards their next destination, they reached the special children school, Neela took the cake box and both went inside the school, the school is for physically challenged, some blind, some deaf and dumb. Neela was moved to tears when she looked at the kids.

Neela placed the boxes and ran away. She could not bear the pain of seeing people in such state. Neela sat on her vehicle, Radha came after distributing cakes. Radha was little mad about Neela's behaviour earlier but when she saw her sobbing in the jeep she felt pity, tried to console her and told her not to worry.

Neela dropped Radha at the hospital and Neela went home and she moved straight in to the bed room and shut the door. Neela never saw such a plight in humans, she was not able to tolerate the fact that god made us all, but why some with disabilities, tears flooded her eyes and her throat choked, she took a glass of water to drink. She tried to relax by resting on the bed. The day passed, Neela packed her bag. It was 4.00 AM. Neela went inside the bathroom to take a hot shower. She was ready for her next destination.

She thanked grandma for the adventure, but grandma thanked her much more and blessed her. She then took blessings from Radha's mother-in-law, kissed Radha's baby and bid goodbye to Radha. Radha's mother-in-law gave her a box with Tiffin and told her to have it on the way, Neela thanked her and she called samba and they bid goodbye to them. Neela started the engine and made it run for a while to get the heat, the rain was not heavy, Neela turned on the music and it was Hare ram Hare ram from Bhool Bhulaiya.

She stopped the music and called Anita and told her she's on the way and ended the call. Neela drove across Polem, came a long bridge called the Kali Bridge across the Kali River. She reached Karwar beach. She drove watching the sunrise, she stopped at a point and took snaps of the magnificent sunrise she reached Karwar city, she drove like a machine she passed Idgundi and then Yellapura, samba was asking for treat. She threw some chicken flavoured dog biscuits.

She reached Mundgod, she was not hungry and she drove continuously hearing music, she reached Chalageri, she crossed ancient ruins of a Digambar Jain temple. Next she came across the toll booth. She checked the mileage and it was 15km/L, Seemed convincing, the THAR has a capacity of 60 Litres, so there is no need to fill up petrol before reaching Bangalore.

She crossed the Tungabhadra River. She was on the Davanagere - Harihar Bypass. She stopped near a field and looked at the time. It was 11.21 AM. She took the box that Radha's mother-in-law gave her, it was Chapattis, she ate them and gave some to samba, samba smelt them but did not eat them, she washed her hands, drank some water and she decided to call Radha. She called Radha but there was no answer from the other side, she must be busy, so she started the engine and drove as hours passed she reached Chitradurga outer. She wanted to have tea, she was searching for a hotel and to the left she found one, she went inside ordered a tea and some samosa, she slammed the jeep door and looked at the map 3hrs to Bangalore.

She drove and she passed Hiriyur, then Tumakuru, just one hour drive to the National Law University.

05

Neela reached the city and was on the way to the University. She looked at the time and it was 4.00 PM. She called Anita and told her that she had arrived, Anita asked her to wait nearby the Jain juice junction. Neela found the landmark on the map and reached the destination. Anita was all smiles on meeting Neela.

"It's been a long time ha?" Anita spoke with a smile.

"Very long," replied Neela

"Two chikkus," shouted Anita.

Neela never had chikku juice before, it was tasty and gruel like, Neela paid the bill restricting Anita to take her purse.

Anita told Neela about the wedding of her friend and asked whether she can be the wedding photographer, the marriage and reception together is 3 days from today.

"So what do you say?" asked Anita.

"My first Wedding Photo shoot, Anita you're awesome!" shouted Neela in joy.

"Control Neela," Anita shouted.

They started jumping holding their hands. Both started back to Anita's home. Neela took a right turn. Anita showed her the route to her home. Anita, a strong modern ethnic woman, doing her masters in the national law university, she was staying alone and she has an apartment near by the university.

The bliss wood residency came. Neela parked the jeep and called samba to follow her, Neela took the leash chain and wore it around samba's neck, samba after getting down urinated on the jeep's tire, Neela shouted at samba, Anita laughed at it, they entered in to the lift and the apartment was on the 3rd floor, Anita searched for the keys inside the hand bag and took them out and then unlocked the door.

Samba entered into the house, pulling Neela inside. Anita threw the key on the table and went to take a bottle of cold water from the fridge. She gave the water bottle to Neela.

She went to the kitchen and boiled tomato soup. Anita came with a bowl full of soup and gave it to Neela and she started to dig in. Anita switched on the TV and the movie The Croods was playing on HBO. Neela made fun of Anita for still watching Animation movies.

Anita fired back by saying that these are the kind of movies which portrays good moral these days. Neela and Anita went out for dinner, Neela was telling about the adventure she had with Radha's Grandma, and Anita was impressed about her grandma and she told she too wished to meet her.

Anita and Radha went to sleep. The next day she had to go to Mysore for the photo shoot. Neela was so excited. She could not sleep at all. It was 3.30 AM. The alarm rang. Neela pushed Anita down and ran in to the bathroom. Anita took bath after Neela. They were all dressed up for the Marriage function.

They reached Mangalore by 7.45 AM and the marriage was held at the Chamundi temple the photo shoot went nice and they had a photo session at the Mysore palace with a special permission, Neela was paid an amount of 10,000 rupees as advance and the photos came stunning, the marriage reception came to an end.

Neela and Anita came back to Bangalore and they went to Anita's university to celebrate New-Year. The whole day she wished all her friends and family, she and Anita were very busy with their phones, calling, facebooking,

WhatsApping, Instagramming. Neela called her uncle in Madurai and told her about her visit and he was very happy and he said everyone in the family was expecting her arrival. She said she will be there for lunch the next day and she spoke to her aunt and their children and wished them all a very Happy new-year.

Neela worked on the pictures of the marriage function. Anita and Neela searched for a photo printer. She printed the pictures in synthetic album and the album came out stunning, Neela got the remaining payment of 10,000 after delivering the album and she gave the money to Anita.

Anita was adamant and was not accepting but Neela kept it on her table. Next day Neela started from Bangalore and drove towards Madurai. She turned on the map and first she wanted to fill her fuel tank, she looked for a pump and then she drove crossing Housr then Dharmapuri. She reached Salem by 7.45AM.

She ate the chapattis that Anita made for her, she came across Karur. She reached Dindigul and finally she reached Madurai. She found her uncle's home and everyone was standing in front of the door to welcome her, the children came running to open the gate for her.

Chapter – 3

The Rekla race

01

Mithun and Ngel were touring in and around Mayiladuthurai and the Navagragha temples. Ngel spent the New Year in Mithun's home. They started off to the south of Tamil Nadu. Mithun got a call from Shobitha, the untold love of his life. She invited him for her marriage and got his address to send the invitation.

Mithun was broke and told Ngel about his love story. Ngel told him not to worry and consoled him that he will find his soul mate soon. As they were visiting Thanjavur, he showed her the college where he studied and the roads where he used to hang out, he took her to the mess where he used to eat everyday and also introduced her to the owner of the house where he lived, then they met Vinayagam at his office, Vinayagam was very happy to meet them and he ordered his worker to get some cool drinks and bondas. They started from Thanjavur to Chidambaram.

Days passed and Mithun's father gave him an invitation and looked at him and asked him when his turn is? Mithun got irritated and took the invitation and ran away to his room. The marriage was to be held at Madurai Meenakshi Amman Temple.

Mithun called his maternal aunt who lived in Madurai and explained about his arrival, Mithun asked about his uncle and her son. He said he is taking a friend along with him. His aunt was very happy on hearing his arrival and asked him to stay for Pongal festival, since it was on the next day. Mithun agreed. Mithun booked train tickets from Chidambaram to Madurai, S7 42 and 43 in Tiruchendur express. The journey time was 6.30 hours and they boarded the train at 8.00 PM. The train started to move.

They ate dinner, Ngel was discussing to the passengers about the superstitions of the country and about her article, everybody went to their respective berths, Ngel on the upper birth and Mithun on the middle, he kept the alarm at 2'O clock and started listening to music through the earphones. The alarm rang he woke up and went to the toilet and washed his face, looked up in the mirror thinking about the marriage, it is a difficult task to attend the marriage of the girl you once loved, he returned back to the seat he took his phone and took the charger out and went to charge the phone. His uncle called him and told him that he'll be there in 20 minutes, he told his uncle to take his time as the train was arriving late.

The train reached the station exactly by 3.00 AM. Ngel and Mithun came out of the station and his uncle was standing near his Bolero. His uncle was the DSP of Madurai. He drove Mithun and Ngel to his home and there his aunt welcomed them both. She gave them coffee. His uncle went to sleep, his aunt and Mithun started to chat and Ngel went to sleep. It was 4.00 AM in the morning, Mithun and his aunt continued to chat. She then got up and went to the kitchen and made tea for her husband and woke him up.

Mithun was watching TV and the time was 6.00 AM.

The marriage was at 7.15 AM. Mithun got ready and Ngel was all dressed up in sari, his uncle dropped them at the marriage hall. Mithun entered the hall, he was scared and upset, he did not want to see her face, his friends came and took him, they were chatting about the old times in college and they were all happy as they met after a short period and their batch mate getting married and it was the first marriage in their batch.

The bride groom was a software engineer from America and Shobitha will be leaving India in a week time, he saw them reciting the Vedas on the stage, Shobitha looked stunning in the red sari, Mithun's throat chocked, he was suddenly surrounded by the mist of misery which was waned away by a laughter, he saw a girl with short hair, wearing a ethnic, bedazzled chudidhar green mixed with bluish color, spreading happiness. She came across Mithun, she was taking pictures of everyone in the hall, everyone was eyeing her and she had a very good camera, Mithun kept a mum face all through the marriage, as the flames were grown on the stage. Mithun's stomach was charring with fumes.

He looked at Shobitha, she was happy. He loved her truly and so he was happy, he understood that moment, that love is all about being happy and importantly your loved one being happy. Mithun was happy that Shobitha got a good bride groom, and he's well settled.

He was sure he could have not given her a life like that, he felt happy and blessed heartily by throwing achatha, the rice grains mixed with turmeric at the groom and the bride. Shobitha tied the knot.

Neela was taking pictures of everyone and then came Mithun and his friends with Ngel. Neela took snaps of them and told Mithun to smile and come a little bit closer, Neela could see the frustration in the eyes of Mithun and took the picture. Then they all went to have breakfast.

Neela was covering the marriage inch by inch, candid photography and she did not miss a gap between the groom and the bride, followed by the video coverage team. Mithun and his friends were having breakfast.

Then they all went to the Madurai Meenakshi temple for getting the blessings from the great god. Neela took a lot of snaps of the bride and the groom in the temple. Mithun wanted to look at the picture and asked her if she could show him the picture that she took, the picture was amazing, it was a low shot covering the bride and the groom along with the temple tower with birds flying and the sun radiating his rays at them through the tower giving radiance to both of them. Mithun was knocked out by the talent.

"Brilliant! I have never seen such a stunning picture," exclaimed Mithun

"Thank you," replied politely and continued to do her work.

Mithun prayed to lord Ganesha sincerely and Neela took a snap of it, and moved forward. Then Mithun and Ngel met the bride and groom and wished them all the best, Shobitha introduced her hubby to Mithun.

"Krishna, this is Mithun, my best friend in college."

"Oh! You are Mithun, Shobitha was telling about you."

Mithun shook his hand and wished him. Mithun and Ngel returned back to his aunt's home. His aunt made him his favorite dish Kootanchoru, he was very happy about it, Ngel too liked it and she was asking doubts about the rituals in the marriage that took place.

02

Neela's uncle, the collector of Madurai also a veterinarian was playing with samba. He came to have lunch at his home. He discussed about the upcoming sport events for Mattu Pongal to Neela and told her that it will be useful for her project. Neela thanked her uncle for getting her special permission for snapping the events. Dr.Pavithran, I.A.S., started to his office after lunch in the old white ambassador provided by the government.

The people's nagging for conducting Jallikattu and Rekla race gave him head ache, as a veterinarian he knew that this a game of animal cruelty, the animals suffer, poor things that don't speak our language. In spite of the pressure from the people and the minister now involved made him to permit the events.

He called the DSP to give heavy protection for event. He invited him to come to his home for Pongal with his family. The DSP wished him.

The DSP reached his home for lunch, he saw Mithun and Ngel at the dining table, he looked at the dish and it was Kootanchoru, his wife went to bring them water and she saw her hubby coming, she called him to take lunch, he sat there along with Mithun. Mithun praised his aunt for making the best Kootanchoru in the world, His aunt kept a scoop of Kootanchoru on his plate and his uncle told them about visiting the collector's home tomorrow after praying. He told his wife that he's been posted at the sports event that is going to take place on Mattu Pongal so he won't be available for the whole day.

Thothathri, I.P.S. Mithun read the name batch in his mind and asked his uncle whether he could take all of them to the event, his uncle agreed by giving a nod with a blank smile and he left for the office after lunch. The next day everyone got early took bath and prayed to the sun god and Mithun's aunt prepared Pongal.

"Pongalo Pongal," shouted his aunt.

"Pongalo Pongal," the others followed.

They prayed to the sun god and ate breakfast and they started to the collector's home. His uncle drove the bolero and reached the collector's house on the way he bought some Halwa.

The collector and his family were on the front of the house and they were seen to be cooking Pongal with earthen pot.

"Just in time for Pongal," welcomed the collector.

Mithun was surprised to see Neela there. He thought she was a professional photographer hired by the collector to capture the function. He was holding the packet of Halwa and he moved towards Neela. He suddenly retreated as samba came barking right towards him.

Neela called samba and she saw Mithun and smiled at him but he was frightened by the black ferocious beast. He asked Neela whether she had come to shoot the Pongal function.

"No, I've come to eat Pongal," replied Neela.

Mithun was dumbstruck and so he left quietly and stood behind his aunt.

"Pongalo Pongal," shouted everyone.

Neela's aunt gave Pongal to everyone in a palm leaf and then they all went inside the house.

Everyone was served coffee. Mithun's uncle introduced him to the collector, Mithun wished him and Neela was busy talking to Ngel, she invited her to come attend the sport event tomorrow.

Ngel told Neela that they are coming there to watch and have fun. Neela and Ngel walked towards her uncle and she wished "happy Pongal," to Mithun's uncle who was sitting near the collector, then came the children and Neela went along with them. Mithun and his uncle, aunt along with Ngel took leave from the collector and started back home.

Mithun was looking for Neela but she didn't come, he sat on the front seat of the vehicle and looked up through the window. Neela was waving her hand with the other children, Mithun smiled at her and she smiled back at him. The rest of the day was spent by watching movies in the television, rest by sleeping. Ngel kept writing her journal and was learning cooking recopies from Mithun's aunt.

03

The next day was a big day. All were gathered in the big ground waiting eagerly for the commencement of the Jallikattu event. The collector arrived followed by the DSP, there was heavy police protection. The minister then came and gave a speech briefly, waved the flag for the commencement of the sport, and the game began with the bull running madly on the narrow lane and the youths trying to tame it.

There was a huge crowd of people around the narrow lane, the bull being chased went on and on, Neela was on a tower along with Ngel and Mithun, Ngel was looked amazed by the sport, she had never seen anything like it.

Neela was taking pictures of the crowd jeering and going mad. To chase a bull and to tame it definitely needs a great spirit of courage, Mithun thought if he could jump in to action but it was not his sport, after 3 hours of chase a youth from the native tamed the bull and the game came to an end.

The youth was awarded with the prize money. The next was Mithun's favorite sport, the Rekla race. The bullocks were fastened to the race cart and made ready, Mithun climbed down from the tower and took a Rekla cart and was all set to race. His uncle had asked for a cart, Mithun and his uncle had planned it secretly, his aunt was shocked. Neela and Ngel too were awe struck. The Kangayam bullocks were fastened in the cart and Mithun and the other Rekla racers were all set and ready to sprint.

The gun shot was fired and that marked the beginning of the race and Mithun was driving his cart with his full efforts and he was gaining speed, one lap down three more lap to go, Mithun was making noises to make the bullocks to move faster and shaking the driving ropes.

He gained to third position and in the last lap he finished first. The first three were allowed to participate in the final, the next session began and the other three racers were selected. There was gap of one hour, Mithun and the other went to have lunch, he went to water the bullocks and fed them. Neela praised him.

The final was about to begin and his aunt advised him to be careful, while driving. Mithun smiled at her and jumped on his cart. The race was between the six contenders and they were all tough racers.

The sound of the gun marked the beginning of the race and Mithun was leading the race till the third lap, on the last lap he was overtaken by a racer, there was a heavy competition on the last lap, it was between Mithun and the other racer clad in black shirt and white dhoti. They raced on par with each other but then Mithun gained speed and finished first, it was a close win.

Mithun was awarded the prize money and he wished the other guy who came second, he came to know his name was Rangan. Neela praised Mithun, and his aunt was so happy and Ngel too was awestruck by the stunt Mithun performed, she still couldn't believe her eyes.

"You're not normal," she said laughingly.

Everybody laughed at it, and his uncle came and congratulated him for his win. Mithun gave the prize money to his uncle.

He told him to keep it since he earned it and let that be his Pongal gift. Mithun was so happy and called his father and told him about his win his father was happy about it and wished him success. His uncle asked Neela to drop his wife, Mithun and Ngel at his home. Neela took them to her jeep.

"Whoa! You have a jeep," exclaimed Mithun.

Neela smiled and started the engine, now Neela was all spirited up because of the race and she was driving very fast which Mithun could understand, Ngel was sitting in the front seat holding to the seat tightly, Mithun and his aunt at the back seat. They reached the apartment and his aunt made coffee and served them all, Neela said that she'll be taking snaps of Kaanum Pongal tomorrow at the bank of the Vaigai River.

Neela started from Mithun's place and she reached her place she greeted her aunt and was telling her about the day. The next day Neela was at Mithun's place, they all went to the river and she was taking pictures and pictures of Mithun, Ngel and his aunt. They all had lunch together and then she dropped them. She was back to her uncle's house by the sunset.

She was busy in making the portfolio of the festival, she heard his uncle arrive, she told him that she's going home tomorrow morning, she called her mother and informed her. Her uncle told her to stay for a few more days but Neela refused since she has to work. Mithun and Ngel were leaving to Chidambaram on the same day. The train tickets were booked already. Neela left early that morning, she was driving back the same way and her destination was Bangalore.

04

Mithun and Ngel reached Chidambaram. His father took an auto to pick them up. They reached the home.

Mithun's father was making Upma for breakfast. Mithun took off the bed sheet that covered him. He looked himself at the mirror, took the brush and squeezed the paste over the bristles of the tooth brush.

The paste was not too much and not too little, he started brushing his teeth. He turned on the heater and took a hot water bath. He came out with a towel tied to his waist. He dressed up. He went to checkout Ngel, she was still sleeping, he called her and tried to wake her up, it seemed like she was not feeling well. Ngel was looking tired, Mithun kept his hand on her fore head and she was boiling.

Mithun went downstairs and told his father about Ngel not feeling well. His father gave him some money and told him to take her to the hospital immediately. Ngel walked downstairs, his father gave her some tea and an auto was called to take her to the hospital.

Mithun and Ngel reached the hospital. His father followed them behind in his bike. Mithun was holding Ngel, her skin was burning and Ngel stepped out of the auto.

She was so tired, her legs were weak, she held Mithun, and they entered in to the hospital.

The nurse came and took a thermometer placed it in Ngel's mouth and checked her temperature, there was a high reading in the temperature, and she was asked to be admitted.

Ngel was made to lie down over the bed and fluid therapy was commenced, she was very weak. The doctor came in and checked her, gave a series of tests and a prescription with a list medicine, Mithun took them and gave it to his father. Mithun's father went downstairs to the pharmacy to get the medicine, there was a long queue.

Mithun came down searching for his father to get the medicine, he saw his father standing second in line and he reached him. His father got the medicine and gave them to Mithun. Mithun ran upstairs to the ward and gave them to the nurse.

Ngel was resting, her eyes closed. The drug was administered to her intravenously. Mithun's father came and he told Mithun that he's leaving to the office.

His father gave him extra 10000 rupees and he took leave. Mithun was sitting in the chair near the bed, looking at the other patients and their relatives, the doctor came and enquired about the blood results, the nurse replied that they will be available in an hour. Mithun was worried and was enquiring about Ngel's health to the doctor.

The doctor told Mithun to wait since the blood results have not come. She tentatively told him that it could be dengue and told him to wait till she gets the blood result. Ngel was undergoing the fluid therapy, there appeared to be rashes on her body.

The doctor came with the blood result and told Mithun to shift Ngel to intensive care unit, and to make arrangements for platelet transfusion.

Mithun called his father and told him about the condition, his father told him he'll drew money from the bank and come there.

Mithun's father reached the hospital, platelet transfusion was done to Ngel. His father told him to go home and have breakfast with a smile on his face. Mithun went home. Mithun's father sat outside the ICU ward, Mithun arrived and sat near his father. The doctor told them that the condition will improve definitely.

Mithun was worried and scared. All he can do is to pray for Ngel's health to recover soon. Mithun slept in the hospital that day his father came the next day, he looked through the round window on the ICU door and Ngel was sleeping peacefully, Mithun kept his palm on his father's shoulder.

05

Neela reached Anita's apartment in Bangalore, she was getting up from the bed. She heard Anita saying that breakfast is hot and it's in the dining table. Anita left for college.

Neela was munching on the breakfast and was looking at the pictures of the Rekla race, particularly Mithun, she was blaming herself for not getting his phone number, he should have asked it, she thought, "Why am I even thinking about this right now" she spoke to herself.

She went inside the kitchen to make a cup of coffee and she was standing in the balcony and thinking, her phone rang suddenly, she rushed to get it but it was disconnected before she could come and get it. She took the phone and looked at the number.

It was a new number, she wanted it to be Mithun, she was in a fix whether to call back or not, what if it was not him. The phone rang again it was a women; Neela sighed and said "Hello, who is this?"

"Hello, I'm Anita's friend Sruthi."

It was Anita's friend's friend who wanted Neela to do a photographic session for a birthday function, Neela agreed and she wrote down the address. The birthday party was tomorrow. Neela wanted to checkout Bangalore so she fed samba and she went to take her jeep out of the parking area, locking the apartment. She went out and she drove near adugodi signal, there was a big college a national university, National dairy research institute. She wanted to drink coffee. She found a shop named Bharathi refreshments. She took a u turn and parked her jeep in front of the shop.

The hotel was a self service kind and upstairs had a dining type of hotel. She ordered a cup of coffee and she was given a bill, she paid 10 rupees.

The coffee stall was neat and there was a name on it saying Cotha's coffee, ground and filtered, she saw the glasses neatly arranged in the tray, she gave the bill to the man and he took the bill and placed it on the hook. He then poured the coffee decoction and mixed it with the milk, the little glass which was white now filled with the coffee was handed to Neela.

Neela took a sip of the coffee, and the sip almost told her how nice the coffee tasted. She found the forum mall and she went inside to check it out.

She wandered for a while, she saw the landmark book section, she entered in and started looking at books, there were lot of books, she really liked TinTin and she wanted to buy the episode the prisoners of the sun.

It was the main inspiration for her to become a photographer and to raise a dog. She billed the book and went upstairs by the elevator, she wanted to see Night at the museum, the theater was IMAX, she called Anita if she could see the movie tonight, Anita told her that they could watch PK instead, Neela agreed and she booked two tickets for the movie PK. Neela was so excited to see the movie PK she returned back to the parking area, she paid the parking bill, which she felt was too high. She drove across the Bangalore traffic, listening to the songs, the traffic was so heavy, by the time she reached the apartment she was very tired and went directly to the bed. Anita came back at 4.30 PM.

She saw Neela sleeping in the bedroom, she went to the bathroom to fresh up and then to the kitchen to make coffee. She attempted to wakeup Neela but Neela was in deep sleep she placed the coffee cup on the table near the bed, Anita held Neela's hand and pulled it. Neela retracted her arm back murmuring something, Anita heard the name of Mithun, Anita's face lit up and woke her again, this time Neela rose and sat on the bed.

Anita was asking who Mithun was. Neela kept both her palm over her face and exhaled. She looked at Anita like she never mentioned anything. She looked at the clock and took the coffee cup, got up from the bed, Anita wanted to know, so she kept nudging her, but Neela kept mum, Anita lost interest, and she changed the topic about the movie.

The show timing was at 7.00 PM. They thought of getting there early so they could have some fun in the mall. Samba was asleep and Neela kept him a bowl of dog food and water.

Neela and Anita roamed around the mall. Anita saw the "Penn store" which was full of pens. She always liked writing with fountain pens. She was looking at the pens through the window and they cost a lot, she was angry about the very high cost, she liked writing a lot, she always felt that writing with a fountain pen explains one's personality. She believed that people who use fountain pens are more reliable and can be trusted more. They are pretty good for long term relationships and people of stable mind and character.

She was immersed in the beauty of the Ganesha carved pen which coasted a fortune, she walked back and she hit someone and asked for pardon. Neela was smiling at her and she held her hand and they got on the escalator. Then they stepped in to the movie hall.

06

Mithun was sitting in the hospital watching Ngel. She was still resting, undergoing fluid therapy. The nurse came there to change the fluids. He saw his father coming with dinner. He took the parcel from his father and went to the canteen to have his dinner. Mithun's father left the hospital, Mithun after finishing his dinner came back to the room in which Neela was admitted, he sat near the bed and started thinking about the time in Madurai, his untold love getting married, but then his mind kept coming to Neela and his heart seemed to be in a blissful state. He blamed himself for being a coward for not asking her phone number. He slept thinking of her,

The sun was shining Ngel was slowly opening her eyes and saw Mithun sleeping on the floor near her bed. She sat up and called out Mithun's name; he woke up and saw her.

"Are you all right?"

"I feel just okay."

Mithun was happy that she is feeling well. She was kept in the hospital for a week to recover.

She was discharged, she paid the money and she moved to Mithun's home.

Ngel was packing, she told Mithun that she was feeling homesick and wanted to go back home. Mithun called Vinayagam and told him to book a plane ticket to U.S.A. Ngel thanked both Mithun and his father for taking good care of her when she became sick.

She got blessings from Mithun's father in an Indian traditional way and they all went to have breakfast. Vinayagam called and told Mithun that the ticket has been booked for tomorrow early morning at 4.00 AM tomorrow, so they decided to drop Ngel at the airport, they started from their home at 11.00 AM.

Mithun was driving the car and his father seated near him on the front seat, Mithun felt wonderful, he felt it was the right time show off his driving skills, but whenever he tried to speed up, his father would tell him to go on an average speed and would tell him about the mileage etc. In an hour they reached Cuddalore.

The east coast road was well laid. Mithun was maintaining his speed on an average of 60/kmph and the ambassador was sailing like a ship. Ngel was asleep. He saw a milestone, Pondicherry 15 kilometers. He drove at the same speed. His father seemed to be satisfied with his way of driving.

The car was entering into Pondicherry and Mithun's father told him to stop at a good hotel so that they can have lunch, Mithun was driving slowly, he was looking for a hotel and then came hotel Sangeetha, Mithun's father told him to stop there and he woke up Ngel. Ngel was tired and she was yawning. Mithun parked the car and opened the door for Ngel.

They went inside the hotel and his father asked what Ngel would like to eat, Ngel said she would take Naan.

Mithun and his father ordered for meals and Ngel got Naan. They started from Pondicherry at 1.28 PM. Mithun was driving slowly and he felt sleepy but still the urge for driving did not let him. At about 3.15 PM they entered Mahabalipuram.

They visited the shore temple they took many snaps and they also enjoyed the beach. Ngel was having a good time with them, she was feeling happy, they were then climbing up the small hill, taking snaps at the light house, Ngel was astonished by the monolithic temples, the Pancharatha and Mithun explained about the Arjuna's penance.

They spent a lot of time in Mahabalipuram it was 6.30 PM and Mithun started the car, Mithun drove faster and they reached Chennai in an hour and a half. They were driving in mount road, Ngel said she wanted to watch a movie, they went to Sathyam Theater and she took tickets for the movie Taken 3. The show time was 9.00 PM they decided to have dinner nearby. The theater was good Mithun had never visited such big theaters.

They came out of the movie theater and straight away went to the airport to drop her. After dropping her at the airport his father told him to drive to Besant nagar, Mithun reached Besant nagar and they stopped at a home and his father got off from the car and knocked the door came an old lady, she was happy to see him and Mithun. They went inside and Mithun was shown his room, his father told him he'll explain everything in the morning.

Mithun did not understand, he sat on the bed, shaking his legs and he was not able to think it through.

The sun rose and Mithun's father opened the door and came inside, Mithun was sleeping, Mithun was very tired after the drive and he did not want to wake him up. He looked at him. It was just if he was a baby and felt like it was yesterday. Mithun rolled on the bed, saw his father looking at him, he did not speak to him, his father told him to wake up and get ready.

Mithun was curious to know who the lady was and how he knew her, he told him that she met her during an act of kindness and she works at a dog shelter in the east coast road. Mithun did not get it.

"I'll explain you later, get ready now."

His father threw him a towel. Mithun still confused, trusted his father's words and went to the bathroom in his room to get ready. He turned on the shower, the water was very cold, there were two pipes and one was for hot water and the other cold.

He turned them both and stepped a few inches from the shower, he felt the water with the back of his hand; the water seemed to be bearable. He came out of the bed room wearing the same dress; his father introduced him to the old lady,

"Mithun, meet Mrs. Jennifer."

Mithun looked at her smilingly.

She was an old lady, but full of life, when she spoke, happiness spread like the light that spreads from a candle during the dark night.

She told Mithun to help himself with the breakfast. Her Nokia phone rang, she went to attend the call, she was talking loudly, she seemed to be a happy person, laughing and smiling always. Mithun looked at the hotbox, hot steaming dosas, were stacked, he took the plate and took four from the hotbox and kept it on the plate, there was some Idili podi and oil which Mithun made into a mixture and gave it to his father.

Six more dosas were remaining. He took five and ate them with the idili podi.

He gave the last one to his father but his father shared the last dosa with him.

Mithun started the ambassador, he looked to his left side door window, he saw his father locking the house, his father turned and smiled at him as he came towards the car, he opened the front door of the ambassador and he gave the key to Mrs. Jennifer who was sitting with a big smile in her face.

Mithun looked at her on the rearview mirror and she was pretty excited. Mithun smiled as he pressed the accelerator. The journey was full conversation between Mithun's father and Mrs. Jennifer. They seemed to be very good friends, thought Mithun. Honking at the bus in front as the signal was green, the traffic was heavy and they reached the Marundheeshwarar temple. Mithun's father told him to park nearby. All three went into the temple.

The temple seemed to be a very peaceful place. They came out of the temple, Mithun started the car and after a few minutes of driving, Mrs. Jennifer asked Mithun to take a right turn near the Samsung showroom. The dog shelter was near and the place was filled with lots and lots of dogs. Mrs. Jennifer indeed was a woman of heart.

But Mithun could not tolerate the sound, as soon as Mrs. Jennifer entered all the dogs became calm and they were jumping at her, welcoming her like a long gone kin who had returned back home, Mithun was touched by the gesture of the dogs, his thoughts ran, there was this old women standing in the centre surrounded by dogs, all jumping in joy.

Mrs. Jennifer stood there in her blue floral gown holding her big brown leather handbag, smiling and laughing at the dogs, calling their names out. Mithun was moved to tears of happiness. Then came a guy, fair, wearing a blue jean, woodland shoe, wearing a big bag, Mrs. Jennifer introduced him as Ishan doctor.

"He's the doctor who treats my darlings."

Mithun's father shook hands with Dr.Ishan, he spoke very well.

Mrs. Jennifer thanked Mithun's father and Mithun waved his hand sitting inside the car, his father came back to the car and they started back home.

Mithun saw the crocodile park board and wanted to visit it, his father agreed, after the crocodile park visit, they stopped at Pondicherry for lunch. They reached home; Mithun's father went inside his room to take rest. Mithun started wondering how good his father is with people. He can start a conversation with anyone and become friends in a few words. He felt that his father had the gift of gab.

Mithun was lost in his thoughts, his phone rang. It was Vinayagam. Vinayagam told Mithun about that the Valaikappu ceremony, he invited Mithun and his father to come to the ceremony. Mithun spoke about this to his father.

He asked Mithun to go alone. Mithun and his father took dinner. Mithun had planned to leave early in the morning. Mithun started the blue ambassador by twisting the car key, like a horse neighing. The car gave a sound and started, he wondered, is that why the engine force is measured in horse power, how silly, he thought and he shifted to the first gear and accelerated as the car moved he shifted to the other gears swiftly.

Mithun reached Thanjavur by 8.00 AM. He went straight to Vinayagam's home, it was a festival there. Vinayagam and his wife both have undergone various treatments for a baby and finally they got their precious gift and they thanked god, Vinayagam and his wife Banumathi were very happy, Vinayagam was receiving everyone with an amazing happy spirit. Vinayagam saw Mithun and he hugged him tightly. Vinayagam's eyes moistened, Mithun has always been there to support Vinayagam during the hardest times of his life. Mithun saw Banumathi, she was so happy.

She was clad in a Kancheevaram pattu and her hands were not visible since they were all covered by glass bangles.

Banumathi looked at him and smiled and in return Mithun bowed with his hands folded. Indeed it was a big day for Vinayagam, Mithun helped in serving food in the dining hall, the feel of festivity was on the air and that kept everyone's spirit up all day, people chatting to each and everyone nonstop round the clock, Mithun looked at the enjoying crowd. His thoughts were lost again, is this why our ancestors made such functions and festivals, meeting people in a crowd was always the root for happiness, Mithun's phone rang, it was his father and he told him that he heard that there is recruitment for the post of archaeologist.

Mithun's face lit up and was merrier than before. He had lunch and then he gave the car key to Vinayagam and thanked him for his help and then took the bus to Chidambaram. He sat in the window seat thinking about his career and, he fell asleep.

He reached his home took his laptop and connected to the internet, he entered ASI in Google and the website for archaeological survey of India showed up, he saw the notification, it was for the post of assistant archaeologist on contract basis and this was a shock to Mithun. He thought that he may get a permanent job but then it's worth a try. He sent his CV and other certificates and emailed it to the ASI.

Chapter – 4

The Engagement

01

Neela left Bangalore, reached Goa and stayed there for a night, the next day she started to Mumbai. She reached Mumbai and went straight to visit her mother and father, they were waiting for her and they were asking a lot of questions about her journey.

Her mother gave her a big hug. They were chatting about the adventures she had and they talked about it all over again during dinner. Neela went to sleep with a deep sense of satisfaction. The day was cloudy. Neela woke up late and found she was late for the office.

She made her portfolio and the prints of her photographs and she showed it to her mother. Her mother was very happy about her talented daughter. Neela took her mother's Nano and zoomed around the Mumbai traffic.

She reached the office and took the files she brought with her. She had to climb the stairs as the lift was busy. She was carrying the album and finally she reached the Daya Arts.Inc magazine, she saw the receptionist and enquired, the receptionist connected her to the manager via the extension number and intimated about the project on Festivals of south India.

Neela was called in by the manager. The manager wished her Makkara Sangranthi and then asked her to show the portfolio and the album she made. There were other photographers in the room working on other projects such as covering the Kite festival.

The manager was very impressed by the photographs and was asked to collect the pay slip by the desk.

The manager praised her for the hard work and also asked her if she was willing to work on a project regarding republic day function. Neela was on cloud nine and she readily agreed, he took the landline and spoke on the extension. Then a few people walked in.

"Yasik Abdulla the camera man, Nisha Patel the reporter and Divya Gupta the editor" introduced the manager.

Neela introduced herself as the photographer for the team, all said "Hi" in a chorus sync.

The manager briefed their work and told them they will be provided the train tickets for their up and down journey to New Delhi. Manager pointed at Neela and specifically told her no road trips this time and smiled at her, Neela smiled back and the others looked at her in confusion.

Yasik told they must celebrate for covering the republic day event. Yasik drove an Omni van; Nisha sat in front with Yasik Neela called Priya to come with her, they all went to McDonalds.

They were all excited about the New Delhi trip and they kept talking about the arrival of Obama and the 15,000 security cameras installed in the capital for protection. Neela left home early to get things packed, she called her mom and told her she'll be home soon and she had lunch and she hung up before her mother could react.

Neela's mother was angry on hearing that she had to leave to New Delhi tomorrow. She was waiting for her father to arrive, her mother did not have lunch, Neela compelled her mother that it is all right and she will be safe, two more girls were also coming along with her. She told her that the security is very tight in New Delhi and she convinced her mother by saying that she had gone all the way all alone to Madurai all by herself, so there's nothing to be afraid of. Neela sat with her mother and served her lunch. Her mother finally agreed half heartedly.

Her father arrived late in the evening, he was very happy to hear that her daughter is going to be a part of news coverage mainly on the republic day event, he felt proud of her. He enquired about the departure, he decided to drop her at the station, her mother also agreed to come to drop her.

It was 6.26 AM. Neela's father started his BMW and Neela sat on the back of the car with her mother. Neela felt it is good to be driven rather than to drive.

She kept her head on her mother's shoulder and rested her eyes a bit. Her father parked the car, took the bags and they reached the railway platform. Neela's mother had packed some rottis for whole crew. Priya Gupta arrived with Yasik and Neela introduced them to her mom and dad. Neela verified the tickets A1 67,68,69,70, were their berths, the date of journey 23.01.2015.

Priya called Nisha but her phone was busy, the FZR JANATA EXP departures at 7.25 AM. Nisha was nowhere to be seen. Nisha came rushing at the platform, Yasik ran to help her with the bags, and she apologized for being caught up with the traffic. The train moved as Neela's father and mother departed from the station waving their hands. The team sat on their respective seats, the other to seats 65 and 66 were empty as wells as the side berths. Neela took the rottis and shared it with the rest, Nisha gave some burgers, and they were all munching and chatting all the way.

02

Mithun received the shortlisted candidate list on his mail and was very happy to find his name on the list, he was asked to be in Institute of Archaeological survey of India located in New Delhi on 28th of January.

Mithun logged in to the IRCTC website and tried to book the ticket but they were all on waiting list. He changed the date for 24th and he found a ticket available. He booked the ticket that was available on the Grand Trunk EXP, he called his father and informed him about the interview, his father came home after an hour and he told Mithun he has deposited ten thousand rupees in his SBI bank account, Mithun packed his bag, he took his father's sweater and set of dresses. He also took his bathroom slippers and wrapped it with old news paper. He was all set for the journey. He went on Skype to chat with Ngel, she wished him best of luck. He was very excited and anxious about his first job interview.

He called his school friend Prasanth who lives in New Delhi studying MBA in Faculty of management studies.

He was very happy to hear him coming and told him he'll be there to pick him up.

The train was at 7.15 PM tomorrow night. Mithun called his aunt and shared the good news. He went to the Thillainathar temple and prayed god to give him the hope to pass through the interview, he asked for the strength to be brave.

He sat near the pond there was a ruin near the pond which was closed for the public. He looked at the architectural marvel built by his ancestors, he felt ecstatic. He left the temple and took a town bus to his home.

Mithun reached Chennai by taking the Boat mail EXP, he took an unreserved ticket and luckily the crowd was less. He managed to get a single seat by the window. He placed his bag on top of the carrier.

An old man was sitting opposite to him. He said his name was Paul. He spoke only in English. He said he taught Tamil in a Government school and now that he is retired from work and gave her daughter in marriage, he's visiting his grandson in Chennai, Mithun introduced himself and Paul seemed to know Mithun's father. Paul wished him all the best and blessed him. He reached the Egmore station at 6.45PM. He asked the way to get to the Central station to the vendor selling tea, he started climbing up the stairs and he walked on the very crowded bridge, he saw the electric train arriving into the station and the crowd was rushing more than before, people were running to get into the train.

He saw giant lights and barricades, he saw the symbol L&T, it was for the Metro rail project, he walked down the bridge which had no stairs but steeping down to the ground and he saw a bus arriving "15B" he saw the board, "Central" was mentioned and he took the bus and there was heavy traffic, by the time he got down at the central station it was 7.00 PM. he looked at his watch, he looked at the screen and found the platform number and ran to catch the train, S1, seat 7 he checked the printout of the ticket, folded it and placed it on his pocket.

Mithun ran till he reached the platform, his phone started to ring, he came to his compartment, the ringing of his phone ceased, he took out the phone from his pocket simultaneously the ticket fell from his pocket, he bent suddenly to pick it up, he crashed with a police women, Mithun apologized to her, she accepted the apology and told him to be careful. He unlocked his Nokia 101.

It was his father, he got in to the train and his seat was side upper nearer to the entrance. Mithun sat on his seat and called his father, the phone rang, the police women he crashed previously was standing in front of him, Mithun was shocked to see her, rather confused.

The train started to move and she sat opposite to him. Mithun was not looking at her but he wanted to. His father wished him luck and told him to call him in the morning, Mithun started a conversation with the lady, and he saw her batch and read the name N.Kirthika.

He introduced himself and told her that his uncle is an IPS officer and works in Madurai. The cop girl didn't budge, she was just listening and she went for rounds, Mithun climbed up to his berth and took out the air pillow from his bag and blew air in to it. He finally settled down.

The only thing that kept coming back into his mind is the fear of the interview, he was sure he can make it but still the excitement and his impatient nature made him very anxious like a racer waiting for the green signal to boom. He connected his headphones to the phone and started listening to music to calm him down, he saw the cop girl coming back. He wished her Republic day wishes in advance. She smiled back at him and wished him back.

Mithun closed his eyes and the thought of Shobitha came to his mind but then suddenly his brain pictured Neela and his heart beat was fast. The music did not calm him down. He decided the first thing he is going to do is to get Neela's contact number, but how? He was puzzled. He stretched his brain but nothing seemed to make sense, only his head started to hurt a little.

He tried to sleep, he put the music on pause, he looked at the phone, the time was 11.22 PM. Mithun took off the head phones and slept. He woke up and climbed down, reached to his slippers with his barefoot and he walked towards the toilet.

He washed his hands and then his face and he walked out of the toilet, closing the door. He saw the lower birth but could not find the cop girl, he climbed back again and checked the time and it was 3.00.AM in the morning. India's 66th republic day, the first question came to him was what did I do to make India better? Nothing! was the answer from his heart, it was breaking him, in the reality he cannot do anything about it, all he can do for now is that he can climb back up and sleep, and that's what he did. The train stood still, Mithun woke up, the whizzing sound of the fan and the tea vendors shouting made him get up from his berth, the sun was high up in the sky.

Mithun washed his face and came back, he stepped foot on Nagpur, he was feeling hungry. He saw a railway restaurant but it was so crowded, then he saw some vendors on the platform.

He took a fifty rupee note from his purse and gave it to the vendor and the vendor gave him four Pooris for 20 rupees. The cop girl was not around. Mithun kept the Pooris near his bag on his berth, took the brush and paste and went to brush his teeth. The train started to move, Mithun came back and took the pooris from the top and ate. The Pooris were big and tasty and the masala tasted just fine. Mithun was enjoying the sight through the window. The sound of the train was always unique. He saw the cop girl patrolling. She walked passed him, it is a tough job to be a patrol police on train, the security was very tight as President of the United States was the chief guest of the day.

Mithun thought of calling Prasanth but he thought he'll call him later. His phone rang, it was his father, enquiring about the journey and his food throughout the journey Mithun answered them all and hung up.

Mithun climbed up to his berth and took a nap, the day darkened and Mithun sat on the seat, he bought a tomato soup and started sipping it. The train stopped at Bhopal, he thought of buying dinner and he took a pack of idili, paid the vendor and ran towards the train. He looked at the time it was 7.25 PM exactly.

The train started to move in 10 minutes, the cop girl came to the seat and Mithun got up. She told him to be seated. She had a pack of food. She sat opposite to him and she spoke Tamil.

She opened up the pack of chicken Briyani; she asked him if he want to taste it. Mithun felt happy and told her that he had got idilis for dinner.

"I hate idilis."

"Hmm"

She told him she got recruited recently and she is on Republic Day special duty. She was then asking about his job. Mithun answered her properly. She finished her Briyani and Mithun his idilis, she went to wash her hands, Mithun followed her and as the train jerked Mithun fell on her pushing her towards the door. The door was closed otherwise both were history by now. She managed to hold him, Mithun apologized to her. She took the empty pack and dropped it in the dustbin and washed her hand. Mithun washed his hand and dried it by wiping his hands over his trouser.

"Don't you feel the chill?" She asked him.

"It's ok, bearable."

"Where do you live?"

"I live in Chidambaram, and you?"

"I live and work in Mayiladuthurai."

"Can I have your number?" Mithun Hesitantly asked.

They exchanged numbers; both were exchanging glances at each other.

"WhatsApp me, when you're free"

"I'll call you, because I don't have, whatsApp."

"You should buy a better phone."

"There's no need and I keep it only for talking and I don't use my phone so much for other stuff."

She told him about the android phones and he inspected her mobile, he liked the phone, had a camera, he always wanted a phone with a camera.

"I will think over it."

"Ok, I have to go for my patrol now."

"Goodnight."

Mithun was pondering over what just happened now and was happy inside, may be the loss of his love is making him travel off track, his conscience spoke. He didn't listen as it felt good. The train reached New Delhi and his friend Prasanth was waiting at the platform.

03

Neela was in distress as all her teammates were hospitalized for food poisoning. They ate a lot of junk food. The manager at the Daya Arts.Inc called and he got furious, but there was nothing he could do. Her teammates were all on fluids. Neela went to the canteen inside the hospital and took dinner.

Luckily Neela did not go out with them on that evening, that's how she escaped from the scene. Neela came to the ward after dinner and stayed with them.

Neela got Pratima's apartment key and her car key and she drove to her apartment, Neela took bath and changed and drove back again to the hospital. Neela was watching the live telecast of the republic day broadcasted on Doordharshan, she went back to the hospital. Her teammates looked worried. There was nothing to do about it.

Pratima spoke about her floral shop and the delivery system they provide, Daisy "n" Petals is the name of the company, she told Neela about her success in the business, Neela was impressed by her entrepreneurship. She praised Pratima for being a winner in this male dominated world.

Pratima explained to Neela that the world has changed now it is a not a male dominated world.

04

Mithun was in the campus of Faculty of management studies, the campus was big and so was the hostel. Prasanth told him to feel free and do whatever he wanted, Mithun took bath and got ready, they left for the canteen.

Mithun had to eat Aloo parotta, this was the first time he heard the name of the dish and it tasted very well, they gave pickle and paneer masala along with the dish which also tasted very well.

Prasanth told him to stay inside the campus since it was Republic day it will be tough to go around places. Mithun and Prasanth came back to hostel. Prasanth gave him his Hard disk and told him that it has lot of movies. Prasanth told Mithun that he will be back by lunch. Mithun spent the day watching movies.

Prasanth came back for lunch just in time and told Mithun that he has a presentation to present for tomorrow and his friend messed up with the presentation, he told Mithun that he had to start from the beginning again. They both went to have lunch, Mithun was feeling cold, the lunch was rottis with chawal. Prasanth started working on his presentation after coming back from lunch, Mithun started to watch movies. Mithun felt sleepy and he went to take a nap. Prasanth woke him up.

"It's past 8'O clock."

Mithun got up quickly and pressed the red button on his phone. The time was 8.15 PM.

"Think I slept well."

"Yes yes." He laughed.

"So how's the presentation coming?"

"It's done and it's good."

"Can I see?"

"Yes you can."

Mithun looked at the slides and it was about new ideas for startups, he didn't understand much but the making of the slide was amazing.

"Dei, you should teach me to make presentation like this."

"Ok da, go fresh up now and let's go for dinner."

Prasanth was tired, he slept soon after dinner. Mithun was unable to sleep, thinking of Kirthika and what he could possibly do if he met her next time.

"Mithun wake up, let's go and get a cup of coffee."

Mithun saw Prasanth all dressed up in his sweater, Mithun got up from the bed took his brush from the bag and searched for the paste, irritated he searched the bag again, he had to take everything out and finally he found the paste, squeezed it on the brush and went inside the bathroom. He came back kept the brush on the washbasin for it to get dried. Mithun and Prasanth went to have coffee; they came back to the VKRV Rao hostel. Mithun wanted to visit places in Delhi and so he got some advice from Prasanth.

Prasanth dropped him at the Vishwavidyalaya metro station, Mithun had never been on a metro train before, he collected the ticket from the counter and he got a small plastic carom coin which he had to show at the gate so that the bar opens up letting him in. He found the way to the platform, it was like as in the movies, the train came and the doors opened automatically, Mithun got in and looked around, it was a bit crowded, he could see the entire length of the train from the beginning to the end. The train moved pretty fast. Central secretariat was the next stop which was announced. Mithun got down and came out of the metro. He had to insert the plastic coin inside the toll. He thought of taking it with him as a remembrance of traveling in metro train, his first experience in metro train he thought walking towards Udyog Bhawan Metro station, he took the bus 980 to India gate. He came across Nirman Bhavan, Archaeological survey of India, he was lost in thoughts about the interview, Jawaharlal Nehru Bhavan passed and the road was called Maulana Azad road, he was observing everything and then came the residence of Vice President, the bus dropped him Near C-Hexagon road, he walked towards the India Gate and his veins were gushing with patriotism, he saw the India Gate and the soldiers there standing in position, he went around the structure.

He heard someone calling his name, may be an illusion he thought and started walking, but someone caught him by his shoulder and Mithun was shocked to see Neela.

"What a surprise!"

Neela was gasping for air, he looked at her and she was wearing a grey T-shirt and a Blue jean with sneakers. She looked stunning.

"Hey, you there?" she waved her hand across Mithun's face.

"Yes, I was just surprised to see you." He stressed.

"Same here, give me a pose for a picture."

"I was just blaming myself for not bringing my camera and here you are the brilliant photographer sent to photograph me."

"That's some coincidence"

"How come you're here?"

"I came here to see the republic day parade."

"Wow!"

"But, my crew members got sick and no parade."

"That's sad, what happened?"

Don't know food poisoning, I guess."

"Are they ok now?"

"Yeah, it was very boring to sit in the hospital, so I thought of just snapping some pictures and here you are!"

"I have an interview tomorrow."

"Good!"

"I am kind of anxious about it, since it's my first interview."

"Oh, then we can try mock interview for you." I'll be the interviewer and you'll be the interviewee.

"Sounds good to me."

"Let's go grab some golgappas."

"Sounds even better."

Mithun and Neela walked around they took an auto to Sarojini nagar Mithun paid for the auto but Neela insisted to share the money. Mithun did not take the money that Neela gave him. They were at the Sarojini market, all kinds of stuffs were there, Neela bought him a Tag Hauer watch and a Raybaan sunglass, Mithun was shocked about the pricing, they were so cheap, Mithun got her a hand bag, it was totally green and Neela loved the color green.

They were talking about their favorite colors to favorite food and they ended up in the golgappa shop. Mithun tasted the golgappas for the first time, it felt really tasty the sour and spicy that filled his mouth, the pooris were big and they were filled with mashed potato filled with spicy sour liquid and they had to open their mouth wide open to push it inside, the crunchy pooris tasted well with the mashed potato and the spicy liquid. They ate 2 rounds and Mithun was full already. They roamed around for a while and they decide to go for a movie, PK Neela suggested, Mithun heard the movie was good, he agreed. They took an auto to PVR cinemas and the show was at 3.45.PM they still had time so they roamed around the mall and they went inside the cinema hall, Mithun was completely awestruck by the concept of the movie, Mithun was discussing about the movie's concept with Neela and they both agreed and arrived at the same suggestions.

They came out of the movie hall, it was 8'O clock and Neela wished him luck to perform well in the interview tomorrow. Mithun took Neela's number before they parted ways; Mithun took the metro to reach the hostel.

He saw Prasanth brought him dinner. Mithun slept after dinner, dreaming about his big interview tomorrow.

05

Mithun reached the ASI early and he looked at the other candidates applied for the same post. People nearly from all of India were there. Mithun looked handsome, he was wearing a white full hand shirt, a black pant and he wore the watch presented by Neela and the glasses were in his pocket.

He was looking at his new black shoes and corrected his black tie. The interview was at 10 AM there was still time, Mithun felt anxious and went to the empty his bladder.

He felt relaxed. He did not speak to anyone, the others were glancing at him, he didn't mind. Then they were all called for the interview. Mithun spoke to the board of members in the interview hall politely and he answered most of the questions.

There was a question about his native, about Chidambara Raghashiyam from the chairman of the interview committee. Mithun explained about the fifth element and about omnipotent being. The chairman was happy with Mithun's answer and he was asked to leave.

The candidates were informed that they will receive a personal mail regarding their selection and they were asked to disperse.

Mithun was excited and called his father and told him he performed well and then called Prasanth. Prasanth told him he is on his way to pick him up, they had lunch together. Prasanth could feel from the looks of Mithun that he did well in the interview. The return journey by the Grand Trunk EXP and Mithun packed his bags and chitchatted with Prasanth, Prasanth dropped him at the station. Mithun called Neela but her phone was busy.

Mithun found his train and walked towards his compartment, he looked at the ticket, S3, 11. He placed his bags on the upper berth, there was a big family seated already occupying the all the seats, he was the only alien in that row. He took some rottis and sat on the corner of the seat, people and vendors were moving to and fro across the narrow passage.

The train started from Delhi, his phone was out of charge and he did not know what to do. He kept the phone inside his bag and slept. He reached home on 30th morning and he took a bus to Chidambaram, he reached his home by noon.

His father was worried and Mithun explained about his phone and the charger that he forgot at his friend's hostel. Mithun thought of buying an android phone. He called his friend and told him reached home safely. Mithun asked his suggestions for buying an android phone, Prasanth told Mithun to check in Flipkart.

Mithun checked out Flipkart and he found the perfect phone for him Karbonn android one sparkle V, he ordered it and opted for cash on delivery. Mithun called Neela and told her that he forgot his charger and his Phone switched off, so he couldn't call her.

He told her that he had ordered for an new phone in Flipkart, they started talking about food and other stuff, Neela spoke about the upcoming photography festival in Goa, she told him that she would go on a road trip, Neela told him that she reached home on the next day, by taking a flight to home since it was very boring there to be alone. Neela heard her mother calling her so she said goodbye to Mithun, Mithun hung up.

Mithun opened his laptop and checked his mail.

"Yes yes!" He screamed in excitement.

Mithun was selected for the job and he was asked to report for duty in the ASI office in Thanjavur. Mithun was so happy that he knew the place very well and he's coming back to the same place he did his post graduation. Mithun called his father and told him the happy news. He called Vinayagam and shared his feelings, Vinayagam was very happy. He called his uncle and aunt, they blessed him. He called Prasanth and thanked him for his help. He called Neela and told her how excited he was! He called everyone he knew, but then Shobitha crossed his mind.

06

Mithun went to Thanjavur on 1st of February and stayed at Vinayagam's home. Mithun had a good sleep and his fears over reality had been overcome. He started to see the day with more enthusiasm.

Vinayagam drove him to the office and Mithun was a familiar face, he was asked to be seated and then came the chief Archaeologist and Director, he congratulated, shook his hand and smiled.

He assigned Mithun to assist in the renovation work done in the Tranqubar fort and told him that his accommodation had been arranged, Mithun thanked him and then he went straight to his university and went to meet his guide, his guide blessed him to attain more success in life and Mithun took a selfie with his guide with his new phone.

Mithun started WhatsApping Kirthika. Mithun packed his stuffs and reached Tharagambadi, his work place was near the beach, the Danish fort stood on the shores of the ocean, it looked majestic. Mithun was taken to his accommodation, the house was pretty good and it was a 1BHK house and Mithun settled well, food was the main problem, the solution arrived soon as one of his colleagues showed him a house where an old couple ran a hotel and Mithun ate there every day. Mithun and Kirthika decided to meet in Sirkazhi. Mithun reached Sirkazhi, took a Kinetic Honda from one of his school friend and went to Sirkazhi bus stand, Mithun could not wait. He saw Kirthika getting down from the bus. She was wearing a blue floral printed white chudidhar.

She saw Mithun and waved her hand at him. Mithun walked towards her and took her to the Tharagambadi fort and showed her around and they became very good friends. He dropped her off at the bus stand.

07

Neela was asleep, her phone rang. She took her phone with an irritated look and she swiped it and kept it on her ear. She heard her friend Shangari talking, saying that her engagement and marriage were fixed and she wanted her to come to Chidambaram soon.

"Chidambaram!" Neela exclaimed.

"Yes that's the native place of my Hubby."

Shangari told her the details and hung up. Neela wanted to attend the photography festival so much but then Chidambaram is more fun she thought. Mithun will be there. That's the first thing that came to her mind. She sent a message in WhatsApp to Mithun.

Mithun woke up with the sound of the message, he thought it would be from Kirthika, but to his surprise it turned out to be from Neela. Mithun replied immediately. Series of texts were exchanged. Both faces had a smile of happiness. Mithun totally forgot about his work. Neela still sat on the bed. Time was past 11.00 AM.

Mithun felt hungry so did Neela and they said that at the same time. They decided to speak when they meet in person. She took a flight to Trichy, she called Shangari to come and pick her up in the airport, Shangari sent her cousin Vikram to pick her up.

Neela sat on the back of the car, Vikram drove and reached Shangari's place. The wedding was fixed on Valentine's Day. Shangari welcomed Neela and introduced her to the in-laws and then to her Fiancée. "Dr. Gemini, a senior research scientist in Defense Research Organization (DRO)." Shangari boasted.

He smiled at Neela.

"My Fiancée is Nuts". He said to Neela.

Shangari acted like she was mad and hit Gemini on his shoulder. Shangari then told Vikram to take her to the wedding Hall for her accommodation.

Vikram dropped her at the wedding hall. This hall was for the reception. The wedding will take place in the Chidambaram temple, Neela heard this piece of information from people talking in the hall. Neela and Mithun started texting each other. Next day they reached Chidambaram temple by 7'O clock in the morning.

There was a huge crowd, the bride and the bride groom clad in traditional dresses exchanged garland and then the groom tied the sacred thread around the bride's neck. Mithun came by the temple. He saw Neela and waved his hand, Neela's face lit up and she smiled in such a way that Mithun was flattered.

The lunch was served in the temple and they waited for the special puja, and the time was 3.15 PM.

Mithun took Neela to his home, the house was his ancestor's and it has come along from generation to generation. Neela felt a sense of ethnicity. Mithun introduced Neela to his father. His father made tea for everyone. Mithun told his father that he's going to take dinner with Neela. He will be back after leaving Neela at Thanjavur.

Mithun took his father's vehicle. Neela sat behind, Mithun rode to Pichavaram, the sun was setting and it was getting dark. Neela asked him a thousand times where he was taking her.

"It's a Surprise."

Finally he made her sit on the motor boat and he drove into the backwaters of the mangrove forest. The trees were like an elliptical cave wall, Neela was busy taking pictures in her phone. Mithun stopped the boat. Neela turned and looked at him.

"I love you." Mithun said plainly. Neela was surprised and stood like a statue. She was speechless, Mithun looked at her state and patted her back and Neela came back to senses.

Mithun once again said those three magical words. He took a cake from the case in the boat on placed lit candles in top of it. It read "I LOVE YOU NEELA". Neela was swept off by Mithun's proposal, hugged Mithun and whispered in to his ears "I Love you too." Mithun took his phone out to take a selfie and both the cheeks near to each other. Mithun kissed her, Neela was shocked by the sudden move and Mithun made fun of how hilarious she looked in the picture. Irritated, Neela took the cake and smacked it over Mithun's face, both lost balance and Neela fell over Mithun. Both lay motionless. Neela heard Mithun's heart beat, it was pacing fast. Mithun was licking the cream on his lips. He took Neela's head in his arms looked deep in her eyes and kissed her fore head.

Neela's phone rang, it was Vikram, and he told her that they'll be leaving to Thanjavur by 8.00 PM. She scooped some cream from Mithun's face and tasted it. Mithun got up and wiped his face. He drove the boat back to shore. He took Neela back to the hotel. Neela bid goodbye to him.

Mithun came back home and told his father about his love and his father was happy for him.

Mithun on the next day went to his work place, Tharagambadi fort. Weeks passed and the love for

Neela grew stronger day by day. His father visited him on Sundays. One day while walking on the beach he found a seal with the symbol of a strange looking object which resembled a disc like object. He decided to check underwater, he called the divers but there was nothing to be found.

He decided to talk to ASI. He was called to undergo training in underwater archaeology, Mithun was not interested but it was in Mumbai, he'll get a chance to see Neela, so he decided to go to Mumbai.

Neela picked him up from the airport and made his accommodation in her flat. Neela stayed with her parents. Mithun enjoyed staying there, she introduced him to her parents and they liked him very much. After underwater training Mithun was given the equipments to explore deep sea and certified for underwater archaeology assessments. Mithun's dad visited Mumbai and they spoke of Mithun and Neela's wedding.

Neela's mom and dad took care of the Astrology chart matching and fixing the date for engagement and wedding. Mithun and Neela got married at Kalahasthi temple. The reception was grandly held at Mumbai. Neela and Mithun lead a happy life. A year passed Neela and Mithun loved travelling and they ventured in the great Himalayan race and they did quite well. They travelled in the path of life like one soul with two bodies.

Mithun and Neela gave birth to a daughter and named her Virupaksha. Neela went to Mumbai, to visit her mother and she needed her to be there to be taken care of her baby. Mithun visited his father every Sunday and spent the whole day with him talking, dining and walking with him. His father was acting strange and one day he told Mithun to pack up his bag pack.

"We're leaving for Spain." His father said plainly.

"Spain!" Mithun's eyes widened and looked at him with great surprise.

Chapter – 5

The Surprise Gift

01

Mithun and his father reached Chennai international airport, Mithun contacted Neela and told him about the visit, Neela was already informed about the trip. She seemed to be calm and Mithun was dying out of curiosity.

Mithun's father did not disclose anything; Mithun looked at the tickets.

Economy Class MAA – BCN Qatar airways, he was ridiculed and they didn't have seats on the same row.

"Why Barcelona"?

His father didn't speak a word, Mithun got angry and frustrated,

"I am not coming." He said as he stood up from the seat in the waiting hall.

"It's going to be your loss" his father looked at him with a smile.

Mithun knew his father is full of surprises and so he decided to stay calm and follow his father.

The flight was at 3.45AM, it was 2.00 AM, Mithun waited calmly, he saw his father taking a nap, he thought he could call Neela, ask her what his father was up to but he looked at his watch and decided not to call her.

He looked at the ticket again, one stop at Doha. It was a long layover. Mithun thought his father will tell him sooner or later. Mithun and his father boarded the flight. They were seated in different seats and Mithun sat near a kid she was playing her PSP, the hostess came and told them to buckle up their seat belts since the flight is to takeoff, Mithun watched the kid fastening her belt and Mithun imitated her.

He saw an old lady seated in the window seat looking tensed as the flight took off, Mithun felt a strange feeling, he held to the seats tightly. The kid laughed at him and told him that he is as afraid as her grandmother is. He looked at her silently and smiled at her. She took her PSP and started playing. Her grandmother was sleeping. Mithun asked her name and she replied hurriedly, since she was busy playing the game

"Fatima." She said looking at the screen as her hands were moving rapidly pressing the buttons on the device. Mithun leaned to look in to the screen but Fatima hid the screen and left out a naughty smile.

Won't you show me?"

"No." Fatima whispered.

Mithun forgot about his trip and started chitchatting with the kid. He felt tired. He put on his blinds and slept. It was a four hour journey. Touch down at Doha. Mithun said good bye to Fatima while collecting his luggage.

"Seems like you made a friend ah?" asked his father. "Yes."

He looked at the watch there it was 5.55 AM, Mithun looked at his watch and it showed 8.25.AM, Mithun's father cleared his doubt by saying that time in Chennai is nearly 2hours 30 minutes ahead of that in Doha.

Mithun nodded and changed his time to the local time. Mithun and his father roamed around the airport.

Mithun thought of asking once again but he did not have the heart. He simply followed his father, he saw a big board "Hamad International Airport", and the airport had an amazing look. Mithun was looking around the airport. They both went through the customs and immigration and checked out of the airport. He waved his hand at a taxi and got in, Mithun followed him hurriedly. He wanted to ask him where they were up to now.

"*To Fraser Suites.*" His father told the driver, the driver started the car and drove off. Mithun looked at the airport mosque that was there. The taxi moved at an average speed, it was moving on the *F- ring road*, the roads were wide and clean, and there were separate paths for cycle and people were riding cycle. The taxi took a long right turn to catch the *Ras Abu Abboud Expy*, Mithun saw the oceanic view and the stretching coast, and he tried to read *Al Croniche Street*, with slight difficulty he pronounced it. The car was moving towards the port and it took a sharp left and entered in to the *Al Meena* Street. The car climbed a slope, the entrance of the hotel. Mithun looked at the hotel in an awestruck manner and hit his head over the glass window.

Mithun got down and took the luggage, his father cut the taxi and put his hand over his shoulder and took him inside the hotel, the gate was opened and the receptionist spoke to his father about the reservation, Mithun and his father took the lift and entered in to the room.

Mithun stood amazed. His father told him to sleep for a while. Mithun woke up hearing his father calling his name, he looked at his watch it was 10.00 AM already. His father told him that he is going to the spa and took a towel and threw at him and told him to freshen up and come down to the spa.

Mithun looked at him strangely, how he changed so much he questioned himself. He changed in to tees and shorts and reached the spa. He saw his father lying down on his front and being massaged, Mithun went inside the steam room, he sat with the towel tied around his waist and the steam was building up and Mithun felt very good and it had a pain relieving effect.

Mithun saw his father swimming in the pool and joined him. Mithun thought about Neela and went to the room to get the Phone. There were 10 missed calls on the phone screen, Mithun called Neela and told her they have reached safely and then they spoke for a while.

Mithun's father entered in to the room and he called Mithun to have lunch, Mithun cut the phone and followed his father. They walked on the Croniche street and reached the Museum of Islamic arts and they roamed around inside, Mithun was immersed in its architectural marvel, he looked at the artifacts, ceramics, manuscripts and textiles and he told himself how beautifully man lived in the past creating such wonderful art.

Mithun and his father walked around every corner of the museum. His father took him to the fifth floor were they reached the restaurant called IDAM, the restaurant looked posh, Mithun and his father took their respective seats over a dining table along the sea view. Mithun saw the menu he waited for his father to order, his father ordered Roasted apple with cardamom and walnut and Labneh'Fontainnebleau', mango for both. Mithun was surprised by the way he ordered, his father looked so natural. Mithun tasted the roasted apple and walnut and the mango vanilla Labneh, they were delicious.

His father ordered two glasses of SULTANA; Mithun looked in to the menu to see what it was, the menu read white grape juice, orange juice and lime juice, ginger syrup and soda water. After having the grand lunch his father gave his card.

After lunch Mithun and his father returned back to the suite and took their luggage and went straight to the airport by a taxi, he looked at the time it was 12.30 PM the flight to Barcelona was at 1.55 PM they checked in the airport and reached the terminus just in time.

The flight journey was of 7hr and 15m, quite a long flight, lunch was served, Mithun sat near his father, he was busy watching the movie cloudy with a chance of meat balls. Mithun took a nap. Mithun heard the hostess announcing to hold on to your seats, touchdown in few minutes. Mithun woke up looked at his father, he was asleep, and he wiped his face from the wet tissue that was near the seat. The flight landed and his father woke up, it's time to go he said.

02

Mithun and his father got out of the airport; an old Rolls Royce arrived and parked in front of them. This is our ride to home said Mithun's father. Mithun started to shake. An old lady was at the driver's seat.

"How are you Susan?" asked Mithun's father in a happy tone.

"Very good dear." "Hop in and lets go home."

"Come on." He said to Mithun throwing the bags in to the car.

Mithun sat in the car totally amazed and his father having a good time talking to the old lady driving a Rolls Royce, everything seemed odd to Mithun, a man who drove a puny two wheeler now on a Rolls Royce, "what is he hiding from me?", he asked himself.

"We'll reach our home in a little while." His father said.

"Yes yes, a big surprise is waiting" replied Susan laughingly.

Mithun could resist the suspense and there is no way his father is going to reveal it, so he played the waiting game. The car took the route of C – 59 just before reaching Moia, the car then took a left turn entering in to a big vineyard, the vineyard was very big and the other side was covered with big dense trees, Mithun saw an old Manor, looking grand and some costly cars standing in line.

The Royce stood still in front of the manor gate. His father asked Mithun to get down and take his luggage and told him this is also one of his homes, and there is a lot to discuss. Mithun stood in silence.

It was 8.45 PM and Mithun entered in to the Manor he examined the house thoroughly with his eyes and

Susan showed his room, and was asked to attend dinner. Dinner was Indian food, Mithun's father cooked dinner and Susan really liked those Dosas he made.

"So what's this all about?"

"You'll know it tomorrow son, now go take rest, tomorrow is a big day."

Mithun understood his father is a man of great power, he left the dining room and approached to the room he was assigned, the bed was very big and spongy and soft, Mithun slept.

Mithun heard someone knock at his door. Mithun opened the door to find Susan telling him to get ready for the big day.

Mithun did not understand anything. Susan left a black suit for Mithun at the table and told him to change and come soon to the hall. Mithun took a hot shower and he changed in to the suit. He walked down the stairs and he found his father on the couch, with a total makeover, he couldn't believe his eyes, he was clad in a black suit and a blue tie, he looked like a natural.

"Nice suit."

"Thank you." Mithun said.

"Do you like it?"

"Yes totally."

"Ready for the big day ah"

"Yes."

"Let's have breakfast first."

"Come on."

"I have to tell you something, it's a secret."

"I'm all ears."

"In ancient days there was a great event called the "*Rathya* - the chariot race", only selected skilled warriors worthy of their bravery and skill can be a member of that society and given the Title Maha-Rathi."

Mithun listened carefully.

"I was also a member of that society."

"What!"

"Yes."

"Descendent?"

"Just listen."

But what we drove was much powerful and they were meant to fight battles.

"So what does this has to do with this wealth."

"This is all that has been won."

"So that's all about the secret."

"Yes this is for now."

"So why did you not tell me this earlier?"

"Because I wanted you to have a normal life and wanted you to stand on your own feet and now after you did, I've gained confidence in revealing the secrets."

"So this is the big day ha."

They both finished breakfast. The sound of the helicopter was so loud Mithun did not hear what his father told him,

Mithun's father told him to follow him. His father climbed on to the copter and told Mithun to jump in.

"What is this?"

"This is big day we are talking about."

The helicopter took off.

The helicopter in a few minutes landed on Barcelona-Catalunya Circuit.

Mithun got the idea about the big day.

Mithun's father got down from the helicopter and he was greeted by Mr. Smith and he introduced his son to him, they shook hands. The owner of the Kreeda Ratha motorsport company Mithun's father was welcomed by the design engineering team, he introduced Mithun to the team, then to the pit crew and he said to the engineer to reveal the car. The car was rolled out from the truck and Mithun's heart stopped for a minute, the beauty of the black tires that rolled from the slope. Mithun looked at them with admiration.

The car was a light blue tinged white streaked color and it had the name written as KREEDA and had the symbol of Partha Sarathy and the chariot.

Mithun's eyes flowed with tears and he went near the car that was standing majestically, he saw his name written with the country flag. Mithun folded his hands and fell on his knees, his father came near him and made him stand and told him this is his gift.

"It's time for testing the car." Spoke Mr. Smith.

"Yes bring the suit."

Mithun was ready, he went forward to get the race suit which was of the similar color of the car, but his father took the suit from him and told him that he still has to learn to drive and that it's not his turn yet.

"So, who's testing the car?" asked Mithun.

Mithun's father smiled

"Not a chance!" Mithun shouted in disbelief.

His father all dressed up wore the mask and then the helmet and then finally the gloves. He sat on the car and attached the steering wheel and he checked them and then he turned on the engine and revved it up, there was big cheer up.

He shifted the gear and moved the car slowly and then he gained speed and he drove out of the pits and reached the main circuit the car moved in great speed, the first corner, he braked hard to turn and rose to full throttle.

Mithun could not believe his father driving at such speeds, the wind was perfect and there was no drag. His father was taking the 16th turn and he drove in the straight road crossing the finish line, but he went for a another lap over the circuit and this time he managed to finish 4 seconds behind the record set on the lap.

He came out of the car taking off his helmet, Mithun looked at him and he was totally speechless. He debriefed about the car and its performance. The technical director was happy as the car performed well and the car was called as RATHA 01.

"When will I get to ride the car?"

"First we have to get you a super license."

"Ok."

You have to take up carting and show progress and if you do well you can go for GP3 and then if you do well then GP2 and then you can come to F1.

Mithun left out a sigh on hearing this. His father called Mr. Smith and asked about the process of the introduction of the team in F1. Mr. Smith replied in positive.

"Now we only have to get you a FIA Super License, but you have to do all these above mentioned to get the license."

"Let's do Karting.

Mithun called Neela and told about this amazing turn of events and he spoke about his father. Neela was quite surprised too. Mithun's father called him and told him to ask Neela and her parents to come to Barcelona.

He also said he will mail the tickets by evening. Mithun was very happy and told Neela the good news.

03

The next day started in the Karting classes and years passed Mithun rose as a champion in both Formula 3 and Formula 2 and years have run so fast. Soon Mithun became famous due to his driving skills. He was asked to be a part of many teams; he attained the super license from the FIA.

India emerged as a great power at the end of the year 2019. Mithun and his family celebrated the New Year 2020 grandly in Mumbai.

Mithun and his family flew to his Barcelona home and there he and his father raced against each other but Mithun could not win him, his father proved to be an excellent driver. The car version now they drove was RATHA 03 a much better dynamic and stable car than the previous cars.

The revealing function took place in their family vineyard and Neela was introduced as the owner of the Kreeda Ratha Motorsport Company. Mithun held Virupaksha near to him posing with the car and then came his father looking young and dashing, Mithun knew he still had some secrets left in him that he is unable to share with others.

Mithun's mind thought in very different ways but then there were lot of flashing lights which brought him back to the reality.

In the mid of the first month of the 2020 year the F1 calendar for grand prix 2020 was released, 25 teams were participating in 20 races throughout the year, this was Mithun's debut year in the biggest motorsport ever F1 Racing.

Mithun was practicing, Virupaksha and Neela would come to see him racing, Virupaksha was more attached to her grand pa and he taught her how to drive, he used to take her long drives in the sports cars that stood in the house. He used to show her the vineyards and go on horse riding and taking walks with samba, while Mithun tried to bring out the best in the track.

Mithun discovered his passion.

The practicing session between the two team members, Mithun and his father were the best races according to Virupaksha, Mithun always wins the race but he knows his father is holding up for his son and his grandchild.

He really wanted to know his secrets, but at the tracks he forgets everything and he drives.

The month of February, Mithun, Neela, Virupaksha and samba started to Paris on a road trip. They left home after having breakfast sharply at 8.15 PM. Neela drove the majestic looking bluish Land rover, Mithun and Virupaksha were seated on the front seat, samba sat on the back seat like a king.

Neela drove fast and Mithun and Virupaksha were screaming out loud. Samba might have thought that they have gone mad and he too started barking. Mithun and Virupaksha kept quiet and they started laughing at samba, which made samba shy away and he hid his face under his paws. Neela was noticing all these and told them not to hurt her poor boy samba, samba immediately made a panting sound and wagged his tail,

"Good boy samba." Neela shouted.

Virupaksha copied her.

Both Mithun and Neela laughed and Mithun held her palm and looked at her. Neela smiled at him.

"I love you." Said Mithun to Neela

Virupaksha shouted the same and samba barked loud.

"Yes, yes I love you all" shouted Neela with a little bit of tear drop running down her left cheek.

Mithun asked Virupaksha "So what are you going to become after you grow up?"

"I am going to become a photographer like Amma and a racer like you" she shouted in a cute voice swinging her hands. Samba let out a bark.

"I am planning to try out the F1 once." Neela replied.

"God, I thought you'd never ask Neela."

"Really you want me to try Mithun!"

"Yes!"

They crossed Perpignan. It was 10.00 AM.

Virupaksha was asleep.

Mithun kept staring at Neela, Neela made eye contact, Mithun went closer to her and suddenly samba sneezed, Neela lost control of the car for a second and then gained control back.

Mithun hit his head in the side window. Neela looked at him and laughed at him.

"Good boy samba."

Mithun looked at samba angrily but samba was chewing its mouth and let out a yawn.

Virupaksha was still asleep.

Mithun started to talk about his father's secret, Neela listened to it carefully but she was out of suggestions.

Mithun turned the topic on having a another child, Neela's face flushed and said

"We can wait for this season of grand prix to end."

"Yes, good idea."

04

The land rover was clocking miles, Neela drove without breaking a sweat, and they crossed La Cavalerie the time was 11.15 AM. The roads were of less traffic and the plains were very green.

They reached Viaduc de millau a cable bridge, one of the highest, Neela paid the toll and drove along the bridge, Neela did not want to be disturbed from her sleep. Neela stopped the rover on the side of the bridge and looked at the ravishing beauty of the nature.

"Issoire" read the board, Neela checked for the grocery store nearby to get something to eat; she found a super market Distribution Automatique Issoiriene. She got some sweet breads, cheese and mango juices. All were asleep.

She started the rover and drove towards Esso, filled the tank. She looked at the time it was 1.35 PM. Neela asked Mithun to make sandwiches with the cheese and told him to feed Virupaksha.

Mithun made a sandwich and gave it to Neela, she took it in her hand and crunched it and drove simultaneously.

Mithun woke up Virupaksha and fed her with mango juice and cheese, Virupaksha liked them a lot.

"Where are we Amma?" she asked

"We're half way there da Kanna."

"Sandwich is very good."

"Oh, Appa made it give him a big kiss."

Virupaksha kissed him and he told her kiss Neela and held her near Neela, Virupaksha kissed her. Virupaksha and Mithun were commenting on the roadways and the green trees that were moving backwards.

They crossed Orleans and it was 4.00 PM. Neela drove fast she wanted to reach soon, she drove to Paris but was caught up in traffic inside the city and she drove to the Abbatial Saint Germain.

They checked in, their room was perfect and they went out for dinner and then a long walk along the streets of Paris, samba too accompanied them. They had a cup of coffee at a café shop and returned back to the room.

The next morning they were all ready by early and took breakfast and they went to enjoy ferry ride tour on the seine river.

Virupaksha was very happy but she felt bad that they let Samba sleep in their room. Bateaux Mouches was the boat trip called, Neela and Mithun were all smiles. They sat on the upper deck. Virupaksha saw the Eiffel tower and was amazed, Mithun too. There were a lot of other places too but the tower was the one that stood still in her eyes.

That day night they went to the Eiffel tower and Mithun proposed to Neela giving her a diamond ear ring with her daughter alongside him holding a rose. Neela hugged them both and let out her tears flow, to free her heart. They dined at a nearby restaurant.

Samba was taken good care bythe hotel management, the next day they visited Louvre museum, Mithun spent more time in the museum studying.

They were roaming like little children along the streets of Paris eating cakes at the bakeries and drinking chocolate milk.

They had a very good time and they saw all great monuments and Neela took a lot of pictures of Mithun and Virupaksha.

Mithun drove half way towards Barcelona and Neela switched half way and they cherished the ride.

05

Mithun woke up from the bed, he found his father speaking to another young man and he introduced him as the second team member. He was Dane. Mithun knew him from the Japanese Grand Prix. He was from England, he was introduced with Mithun to the press and then the last training sessions and Dane performed well.

Mithun did not understand why his father did not participate but did only the test drives. There were a lot of questions in his mind and he could not think of an answer.

Mithun spent his time racing against Dane, Dane seemed to keep up with Mithun and he was good too. Mithun's father was spending much of his time taking Virupaksha and samba for long walks in to the vineyards.

Neela was always present at the race track cheering Mithun. The start of the grand prix was nearing and Mithun was anxious and all excited. The first race will commence on India in the Buddh international circuit.

One of the best tracks in the F1 Grand prix. The pressure on performing on the home ground haunted Mithun. Neela could only calm him down.

His father did not speak much to him and he was a bit isolated from him and he was busy practicing for the big day. The days were getting closer and the team was transported to the F1 Track, Mithun's father saw him with pride and then shook his hands before the day of the race after he spoke to the Press and media. Mithun came to his room and found a letter and a key as a weight, the key looked similar it was like the Tamil letter "U - உள" with a bit on the end. Mithun took the letter and started to read.

Dear son,

I, your father have lived many years and that has been my biggest secret. It may seem like a boon but it is actually a curse, to see all your loved ones to pass away right in front of your eyes. This curse was the biggest gift I had and it made me understand that humans are still not ready for the wonders of the nature. Do not look for me for my duty is done and do not worry because I cannot die. It is sad that I have to leave you at this point on your big day. But I have to and you'll understand the significance in the later years. Take good care of my grand child and my daughter in law and tell them I'll be back soon.

With love
You're Father
Pasa Chiranjivi
(Near Immortal)

Mithun looked at the letter and fell over the chair reading the letter again and again; he knew there was something supernatural about him. He decided to unearth the secrets after he finish the season. He read the name Near Immortal, he knew his father's name was Chiranjivi but this was the first time he mentioned his full name Near Immortal. Mithun thought a lot about it and he was not afraid anymore, he didn't have the pressure of performing, he became confident and he went back to Neela. She was sleeping along with Virupaksha. Mithun kissed them both and slept near them.

The next day was the qualifying session, Mithun and Dane qualified and took first and third pole position. The crowd cheered. There was a great spirit of nation and pride.

The next day was the race day and Mithun was meditating, Virupaksha and Neela were told that his father had to go to Spain to do something urgently.

Neela too could understand there was something wrong, she decided to ask Mithun after the race day. Virupaksha at the track wishing him luck ran to her mother and Mithun sat on the car, he held the steering wheel and he told to himself "is this for real"

"Yes! Neela told him over the Radio." Both laughed.

Virupaksha wished him all the best over the radio.

He could see the mirage on the road due to the hot weather, he was waiting for the light to turn green and when it did!

Mithun Vroomed.

His father smiled at watching him drive and sang.

"BhO ShambO Shiva SambO SvayambO."

Printed in the United States
By Bookmasters